T0319560

THE NEW LOMBARD STREET

THE NEW LOMBARD STREET

How the Fed Became the Dealer of Last Resort

Perry Mehrling

PRINCETON UNIVERSITY PRESS
Princeton & Oxford

LIBRARY OF CONGRESS CATALOGING-IN-PUBLICATION DATA

Mehrling, Perry.

  The new Lombard Street : how the Fed became the dealer of last resort / Perry Mehrling.

  p.   cm.

Includes bibliographical references and index.

ISBN 978-0-691-14398-9 (hbk. : alk. paper) 1. Federal Reserve banks—History. 2. Banks and banking, Central—United States—History. 3. Monetary policy—United States. 4. Finance—United States. 5. United States—Economic policy. I. Title.

HG2563.M36 2011

332.1'10973—dc22   2010023219

British Library Cataloging-in-Publication Data is available

This book has been composed in Adobe Garamond and AT Chevalier

10 9 8 7 6 5 4 3 2 1

To Judy, the kids, and the grandkids

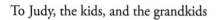

I am by no means an alarmist. I believe that our system, though curious and peculiar, may be worked safely; but if we wish so to work it, we must study it. Money will not manage itself, and Lombard Street has a great deal of money to manage.

—Bagehot (1906 [1873], 20)

Contents

Acknowledgments

This book has taken me fifty years to formulate, but it was Seth Ditchik's query back in November 2008 that finally got me to write it. Given the drama playing out before our eyes, he thought there might be room for a book that would put the current crisis in some larger historical perspective, and he thought I might be the person to write it. I don't know that I have written exactly the book he had in mind, but I can definitely say that I have written the book I had in me. It revisits terrain that I have toured in my previous books, *The Money Interest and the Public Interest* (chaps. 2 and 3) and *Fischer Black and the Revolutionary Idea of Finance* (chap. 4), but the perspective is new. That perspective has been hard-won from experience of more than a decade teaching patient New York undergraduates how the money markets downtown actually work (chap. 5). But it is also fresh in the sense that it has been forced sharply into focus by the events since August 2007, and by my attempt to participate constructively in the policy response to those events (chap. 6). The "money view" that I had been developing in the classroom seemed to make sense of what was happening even when other more familiar views, from economics and finance both, did not.

Above all others, Larry Kotlikoff deserves thanks for arranging my accommodations at Boston University during the year 2008–2009, for pushing me into the policy process, and then for backing off and letting me write the book. Probably I have not written the book he would have liked—he has written that book himself, under the title *Jimmy Stewart Is Dead*—but the book I have written would be quite different, in ways that are impossible to imagine, without him. Thanks also to Joe Stiglitz and the folks at Columbia University's Initiative for Policy Dialogue for making room for my somewhat premature maunderings about credit default swaps back in May 2008, and to Jamie Galbraith and the folks at Economists for Peace and Security for multiple opportunities to present my developing views, first in November 2008.

Thanks also to those, mostly at the New York Fed, who worked tirelessly behind the scenes to create the programs that put a floor under the crisis, programs that I believe show us the road toward a workable future beyond this crisis. It is the nature of their work that I know a lot more about the programs than the people, so they are largely unsung heroes, but heroes nonetheless. Thanks also to my academic colleagues who, beyond the call of scholarly duty, found time in the middle of their own work to read and comment on chapter drafts along the way: Roger Backhouse, Aaron Brown, Andre Burgstaller, Ben Friedman, Charles Goodhart, Rob Johnson, Anush Kapadia, David Laidler, Daniel Neilson, Goetz von Peter, Sanjay Reddy, and Roger Sandilands. Probably all of these—both Fed staff and academic colleagues—will find something to disagree with in the book, and that is as it should be; one lesson of the history I relate is that when academics and practitioners agree, we should worry.

Thanks finally to my family, who made room for yet another summer of Papa In His Study, not excluding even two August weeks in Cortona, Italy, where the first draft of chapter 3 was produced. None of this would have been possible without your lasting support. It takes a family to write a book; you are mine, and this is yours.

THE NEW LOMBARD STREET

Introduction

The financial crisis that started in August 2007 and then took a sharp turn for the worse in September 2008 has proven to require more than the *Subprime Solution* advocated by the Yale professor Robert Shiller, and to involve significantly greater loss than the *Trillion Dollar Meltdown* foreseen by Charles Morris. It is instead proving to be what Mark Zandi has called an "inflection point in economic history." That means that we need a historical perspective in order to understand our current predicament and to see beyond it to a possible future.[1]

The intellectual challenge of producing such an account is large, given the scope of the crisis that is transforming not only banking and financial institutions and markets but also the regulatory and supervisory apparatus within which those institutions operate, including most dramatically the role of the Federal Reserve. On this last point alone, textbooks still teach that the main task of the Fed is to control the short-term rate of interest in order to achieve a long-run inflation target. Ever since the crisis began, however, the Fed has instead been fighting a war, using every weapon at hand, including a number of new ones never used before.

"Lender of last resort" is the classic prescription for financial crisis. "Lend freely but at a high rate" is the mantra of all central bankers, ever since the publication of Walter Bagehot's magisterial *Lombard Street: A Description of the Money Market* (1873). That is what the Fed did during the first stages of the crisis, as it sold off its holdings of Treasury securities and lent out the proceeds through various extensions of its discount facility.

But then, after the collapse of Lehman Brothers and AIG, and the consequent freeze-up of money markets both domestically and internationally, the Fed did even more, shifting much of the wholesale money market onto its own balance sheet, more than doubling its size in a matter of weeks. In retrospect this move can be seen as the beginning of a new role for the Fed that I call "dealer of last resort."

And then, once it became apparent that the emergency measures had stopped the free fall, the Fed moved to replace its temporary loans to various elements of the financial sector with permanent holdings of mortgage-backed securities, essentially loans to households. This is something completely new, not Bagehot at all—an extension of "dealer of last resort" to the private capital market.

The transformation of the Fed's role during this crisis is evident in a simple chart showing the evolution of the Fed's balance sheet, both assets and liabilities, in 2007–2009 (see figure 1). The stages of the crisis stand out clearly, marked by key turning points: the collapse of Bear Stearns in March 2008, and of Lehman Brothers and AIG in September 2008. The chapters that follow are an attempt to provide the historical and analytical context necessary for understanding what this chart means for us, today and going forward.

A Money View Perspective

It is no accident that the Fed has been at the center of policy response. Indeed, a fundamental premise of this book is that a "money view" provides the intellectual lens necessary to see clearly

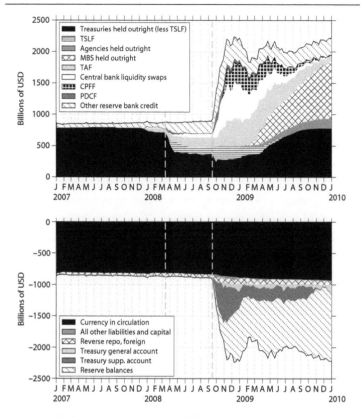

Figure 1: Fed assets (top panel) and liabilities (bottom), 2007–2009. Source: Federal Reserve Board H.4.1 "Factors Affecting Reserve Balances." Online at www.federalreserve.gov/releases/h41

the central features of this multidimensional crisis. The reason is simple. It is in the daily operation of the money market that the coherence of the credit system, that vast web of promises to pay, is tested and resolved as cash flows meet cash commitments. The web of interlocking debt commitments, each one a more or less rash promise about an uncertain future, is like a bridge that we collectively spin out into the unknown future toward shores not yet visible. As a banker's bank, the Fed watches over the construction of that bridge at the point where it is most vulnerable, right at the leading edge between present and future. Here failure to make a promised payment can undermine any number of other promised payments, causing the entire web to unravel.

The Fed does not just watch; it also intervenes. As a banker's bank, the central bank has a balance sheet that gives it the means to manage the current balance between cash flows and cash commitments. "Lender of last resort" is one example, in which the central bank temporarily offers up its own cash to meet commitments that would not otherwise be fulfilled. "Bank rate policy" extends this kind of intervention from crisis to normal times, in an attempt to ward off crisis before it happens. By intervening in the money market, the Fed seeks to offer a bit more elasticity or to impose a bit more discipline, easing or tightening as conditions warrant.

A century ago, at the time of the founding of the Fed in 1913, this "money view" way of thinking was quite common, but today economic discussion is instead dominated by two rather different views. On the one hand, we have the view of *economics*, which resolutely looks through the veil of money to see how the prospects for the present generation depend on investments in real capital goods that were made by generations *past*. On the other hand, we have the view of *finance*, which focuses on the present valuations of capital assets, seeing them as dependent entirely on imagined *future* cash flows projected back into the present.

The economics view and the finance view meet in the present, where cash flows emerging from past real investments meet cash commitments entered into in anticipation of an imagined future. This *present* is the natural sphere of the *money* view. But both economics and finance abstract from money; for both of them, money is just the plumbing behind the walls, taken for granted. Both largely ignore the sophisticated mechanism that operates to channel cash flows wherever they are emerging to meet cash commitments wherever they are most pressing. As a consequence, neither the economics view nor the finance view has been particularly well suited for understanding the crisis we have just been through, a crisis during which the crucial monetary plumbing broke down, almost bringing the rest of the system down with it.

The economics and finance views have taken turns dominating postwar economic discussion. First, in the immediate post–World War II decades, the economics view held sway—understandably so in the aftermath of depression and world war. Private and public sector alike built their present on the foundations of the past, the only solid ground that remained after the dust of war had cleared. Then, in more recent decades, the finance view has held sway—excessively so, as the present crisis now confirms. Private and public sector alike dreamed fantastical dreams about the future, and financial markets provided the resources that gave those dreams a chance to become reality.

As a consequence of this long dominance of the economics and then finance views, modern policymakers have lost sight of the Fed's historical mission to manage the balance between discipline and elasticity in the interbank payments system. In Bagehot's day, the Bank of England understood "bank rate" as the cost of pushing the day of reckoning off into the future; manipulation of that cost by the Bank was supposed to provide incentive for more or less rapid repayment of outstanding credit, and more or less rapid expansion of new credit. No longer. Today policymakers understand the Fed's job to be taking completely off the table any concern about the mere *timing* of cash flows. The money view has been obscured by other perspectives.

Abstracting from money, both the economics and finance views have in effect treated liquidity as a free good and, even more, offered up their theories of such an ideal world as the norm for monetary policy. According to that ideal, liquidity should not be scarce at all; users of the monetary system should be making decisions based on their intertemporal budget constraints, not their immediate cash constraints. Ideally, money should be just a veil obscuring the real productive economic processes underneath, and the job of the Fed is to get as close to that ideal as possible. The rate of interest should reflect the price of time, not the price of liquidity.

Lessons from the Crisis

One lesson of the crisis is that this ideal norm goes too far. Our thinking about money has mistaken the properties of models that formalize the economics and finance views for properties of the real world. This is an intellectual error, but one with significant practical consequences not least because it inserts a bias toward excessive elasticity at the very center of monetary policy. That bias has fueled the asset price bubble that created the conditions for the current crisis, and that bias will fuel the next bubble as well unless we learn the lesson that the current crisis has to teach.

How ever did we lose knowledge that was once commonplace, the knowledge that came from the older money view? This book traces the origin to the well-meaning American economist Harold Moulton who, in 1918, urged the importance of commercial banking for capital formation. According to Moulton, American banks had improved on outdated British practice by relying on the "shiftability" (or salability) of long-term security holdings to meet current cash needs, rather than on the "self-liquidating" character of short-term commercial loans. This change in banking practice made it possible for American banks to participate in financing long-term investment, and that participation was crucial for the capital development of the nation. At the time, Moulton's shiftability theory provided intellectual support for those who sought to break from the conservative bank doctrine of yesteryear, and thus helped to shift the balance from excessive discipline toward more appropriate elasticity, but it also did more than that.

This book tells the story of how the triumph of Moulton's shiftability view, as a consequence of depression and war as much as anything else, eventually led to the almost complete eclipse of the money view in modern discourse. Today policymakers focus their attention on the rate of interest that would be established in an ideal system of perfect liquidity. Instead of monitoring the balance between discipline and elasticity, the modern Fed attempts to keep the bank rate of interest in line with an ideal "natural rate" of interest, so called by the Swedish reform economist Knut Wicksell.[2]

In contrast to those who held the money view, the academic Wicksell did not see any inherent instability of private credit that central bankers must manage, but rather an inherent stability that central bankers are prone to mismanage. According to him, the profit rate on capital is a "natural rate" of interest in the sense that the economy would be in equilibrium at that rate. The problem comes when central bankers choose a "money rate" of interest different from this natural rate. If lower, then the differential creates an incentive for credit expansion to fund new capital investment, and the new spending tends to drive up the general level of prices. Higher prices bring improved profitability and hence also improved creditworthiness, which creates incentive for further credit expansion in an unsustainable cumulative upward spiral.

Wicksell's academic way of looking at the world had clear implications for monetary policy: set the money rate equal to the natural rate and then stand back and let markets work. Unfortunately, the natural rate is not observable, but we do observe the price level, and so we can use that as an indicator of whether the money rate is too high or too low. If prices are rising, then the money rate is too low and should be increased; if prices are falling, then the money rate is too high and should be decreased. Unlike the classic British money view, Wicksell tells us that central bankers have no need to pay close attention to conditions in the money market. They just need to watch the price level.

In modern formulations, neo-Wicksellian policy rules are derived from somewhat different analytical foundations, and they focus attention not on the price level but instead on price inflation as an indicator for policy.[3] But the idea is the same. Central bankers have no need to pay attention to conditions in the money market. They just need to watch prices and adjust interest rates accordingly. One modern formulation of this type is the so-called Taylor rule, which uses the level of aggregate income as well as inflation as an indicator of the appropriate setting for the money rate of interest. The Stanford economist John Taylor has suggested that the origin of our present crisis lies in the failure of the Fed to follow such a Taylor rule, choosing instead to keep the money rate below the rule level for about four years, 2002–2005, thus fueling the bubble that burst in 2007.[4]

Taylor's conclusion that the underlying problem was excessive monetary ease is compatible with the older money view, but the money view would look to developments in private credit markets as well as to actions of the Fed in order to understand what happened. From a money view perspective, instability is the natural tendency of credit markets, not necessarily a consequence of monetary mismanagement; as Bagehot famously stated, "Money does not manage itself." A central bank that understands its role to be the elimination of liquidity constraints, however, tends to exacerbate this natural tendency toward instability because it eliminates a key source of discipline that would otherwise constrain individuals and coordinate their market behavior. The problem we face is not that the Fed failed to follow an appropriate neo-Wicksellian Taylor rule but rather that neo-Wicksellian policy rules are themselves excessively biased toward ease.

Such a bias, it is important to note, would have been impossible in the circumstances for which the money view was originally developed, namely, the nineteenth-century gold standard. In those circumstances, excessive ease would have led promptly to gold outflows, threatening maintenance of gold convertibility in international exchange markets. The breakdown of the gold standard, and its replacement by a dollar standard, meant that the U.S. monetary system faced no such reserve constraint. Here we find further institutional basis for decline of the money view.

The Fed could, of course, have imposed such a reserve constraint on the system as a matter of policy, but in general it chose not to do so. (The Volcker episode of 1979–1983 stands out as the only significant exception.) For that policy choice, the intellectual support provided by the economics view and then the finance view was crucial. Abstraction from the plumbing behind the walls provided scientific support for a policy stance that was at systematic variance with what the older money view would have recommended. Dominance of the economics and finance views meant that policymakers chose from a palette of policy options that was biased toward ease.

That said, release from the excessive discipline of the gold standard was certainly a good thing, and it follows that restoration of the Bagehot-era money view is no solution to the current crisis in economic thinking. Bias toward excessive discipline is no answer to the current bias toward excessive elasticity. Instead, what is needed is a restoration of the ancient central banking focus on the *balance* between discipline and elasticity. Furthermore, because the modern economic and financial world is much changed from the world in which the money view originally arose, restoration of ancient wisdom must be accompanied by reconstruction for modern conditions and concerns.

This book seeks to begin that reconstruction by taking a resolutely money view approach to understanding the recent credit crisis, and by drawing lessons from that crisis for the future. The main lesson is that a modern money view requires updating Bagehot's conception of the central bank as a "lender of last resort." Under the conditions of the New Lombard Street, the central bank is better conceptualized as a "dealer of last resort."

ONE

Lombard Street, Old and New

Writing in 1967, before he had yet formulated his famous Financial Instability Hypothesis, the American monetary economist Hyman Minsky identified the starting point for his analysis. "Capitalism is essentially a financial system, and the peculiar behavioral attributes of a capitalist economy center around the impact of finance on system behavior."[1] From this point of view, the key institutions of modern capitalism are its financial institutions, which make a business out of managing the daily inflow and outflow of cash on their balance sheets. And the quintessential financial institutions are banks, whose daily cash inflows and outflows are the mechanism of the modern payments system.

Everyone else—households, businesses, governments, even entire nations—is also a financial institution since, in addition to whatever else they do, they must attend to the consequences of their activities for their own daily cash flow. Indeed, this daily cash flow, in and out, is the crucial interface where each of us connects with the larger system. This interface provides the cash that makes it possible for us to pursue today dreams for the future that would otherwise be impossible; but it does so at the cost of committing us to make future payments that can, if our dreams do not work out, constrain our independence more or less severely. The seductive allure of present credit and the crushing burden of future debt are two faces of the same creature.

The Inherent Instability of Credit

The two faces of credit show themselves not only at the level of each individual, but also at the level of the system as a whole because one person's cash inflow is another person's cash outflow. If the allure of credit induces one person to increase spending, the immediate result is income somewhere else in the system, which income is then available for additional spending. Similarly, if the burden of debt induces one person to decrease spending, the immediate result is reduced income somewhere else in the system, and thus possibly also reduced spending. This interaction of balance sheets is the source of what the British monetary economist Ralph Hawtrey called the inherent instability of credit.[2] In his view, the main job of the central bank is to prevent a credit-fueled bubble from ever getting started, in order to avoid the collapse that inevitably follows.

But, from another point of view, the inherent instability of credit is not entirely a bad thing. On the way up, real things get built, new technologies get implemented, and productive capacity expands. The Austrian economist Joseph Schumpeter always insisted that credit is critical for the process of "creative destruction" that is the source of capitalism's dynamism, because it provides the crucial mechanism that allows the new to bid resources away from the old. Instability is, from this point of view, inseparable from growth, and a central bank that intervenes to control instability runs the risk of killing off growth by stifling the new on the way up and coddling the old on the way down.[3]

In any concrete case, the question therefore arises: are we looking at a Hawtreyan speculative bubble that we want to rein in, or at Schumpeterian dynamic growth that we want to let run? One reason this question is hard to answer is that a credit-fueled boom typically involves a bit of both. That is why we seem always to be tempted to draw a distinction between speculative and productive credit, and to look for ways to channel credit preferentially to the latter. But in practice the distinction is often difficult to draw and, even more problematic, discrimination in credit allocation is often impossible to implement. In this latter regard, the institutional structure of finance, including the regulatory structure, is crucial. If potential borrowers and lenders can find one another and do business outside the reach of the authorities, then it will be impossible to allocate credit preferentially to socially desirable uses, even assuming they could be identified and agreed on. (In such a situation, even control of *aggregate* credit can be quite difficult.)

In the last analysis, the only dependable source of leverage over the system as a whole is the role of the central bank as a banker's bank. If banks are the quintessential financial institution because of their management of the retail payments system, then the central bank is the quintessential bank because of its management of the payments system that banks themselves use. When one bank makes a payment to another, the mechanism involves changing entries on the balance sheet of the central bank; there is a debit to the account of the bank paying and a credit to the account of the bank being paid. Here, in the requirement to settle net payments every day on the books of the central bank, we find the location of the ultimate discipline for the entire system.

Hyman Minsky called this requirement the "survival constraint"—cash inflows must be sufficient to meet cash outflows—and we all face such a constraint. For banks, the survival constraint takes the concrete form of a "reserve constraint" because banks settle net payments using their reserve accounts at the central bank. The leverage that the central bank enjoys over the larger system arises ultimately from the fact that a bank that does not have sufficient funds to make a payment must borrow from the central bank. In such a circumstance, the central bank must lend or else risk a breakdown of the payments system, but the lending does not have to be cheap or easy. It is the central bank's control over the price and availability of funds at this moment of necessity that is the source of its control over the system more generally.

Opportunities for such control arise naturally from time to time, simply because of fluctuations in the pattern of payments, but the central bank can also create such opportunities as the need arises. Just so, when the central bank "tightens money" by selling Treasury bills, the consequence is that the banking system as a whole has to make payments to the central bank, which amounts to tightening the survival constraint that all bankers face. Alternatively, when the central bank "loosens money" by buying Treasury bills, the consequence is that the banking system as a whole receives payments from the central bank, thus relaxing the survival constraint. The effects of these central bank interventions show up in the short-term rate of interest that banks pay as the cost of putting off to the future a payment that is due today. Historically, the art of central banking was all about the choice of whether to raise or lower that cost.

The central bank's ability to influence the degree of discipline or elasticity faced by banks at the daily clearing provides some control over the credit system as a whole, but that control is by no means absolute. Private credit elasticity is always a substitute for public credit elasticity. In its attempt to impose discipline, sometimes the most the central bank can do is to force banks to find and use alternative private credit channels. Similarly, in its attempt to impose elasticity, sometimes the most a central bank can do is to offer its own public credit as an alternative to collapsing private credit.

That's why Hawtrey referred to the "art" of central banking, rather than the "science" or the "engineering."[4] The central bank can use its balance sheet to impose a bit more discipline when the private market is too undisciplined, and it can use its balance sheet to offer a bit more elasticity when the private market is imposing excessive discipline. But it is only one bank and ultimately small relative to the system it engages, especially so in the modern globalized financial system in which private credit markets are all connected into an integrated whole. Because the central bank is not all-powerful, it is especially important that it choose its policy intervention carefully, with a full appreciation of the origins of the instability that it is trying to counter.

According to Hawtrey, the inherent instability of credit has its origin in the way that credit-financed spending by some creates income for others, not only directly but also indirectly by pushing up the price of the good being purchased, thus producing an upward revaluation of existing inventories of the good. The capital gain for holders of inventories tends to stimulate additional spending, in part to buy ahead of rising demand in order to earn additional profit from rising prices in the future. Because revaluation of existing inventories tends to improve creditworthiness, this additional spending is easy to finance, even easier than the initial spending. The feedback loop of rising asset prices and credit expansion is the source of the inherent instability of credit emphasized by Hawtrey.

The price-credit feedback mechanism is also the reason that credit-fueled bubbles are so difficult to control, because it means that central bank interest rate policy can sometimes have very little traction. The question for the speculator is only whether the rate of appreciation of the underlying asset is greater than the rate of interest, and that is a condition often quite easily satisfied. If house prices are appreciating at 15 percent a year, it takes an interest rate of greater than 15 percent to stifle the bubble. Even supposing that the central bank is able to impose such a high interest rate, 15 percent would stifle a lot of other things as well. Conclusion: if you don't catch the bubble early, it may be impossible to do anything using interest rate policy.

Meanwhile, the larger the bubble grows, the greater the distortion in the allocation of credit and in the allocation of real resources commanded by that credit. Not only does a bubble prospect of 15 percent attract new credit disproportionately, but also it bids up the price of credit across the board. Borrowers and lenders find one another at a rising market rate of interest, and the central bank must raise its policy rate merely to keep up. Eventually, and long before interest rates reach 15 percent, the effects of higher market interest rates are felt on nonbubble balance sheets throughout the economy, and it is these effects that bring the bubble to an end.

The way it works is this. Higher interest rates mean greater cash outflows for debtors, and eventually the most vulnerable among them find their cash outflows exceeding their cash inflows. If you are one of those vulnerable debtors, Minsky's survival constraint begins to bind for you. Logically there are only three ways out. First, you can spend down any cash balances you may have, but these balances are finite and quickly exhausted. Second, you can borrow to cover the shortfall, but credit lines are also finite, and even possibly contracting in the face of declining creditworthiness. Third, you can sell some of your earning assets, for whatever price they will fetch on the market. Typically these three ways out are used sequentially, as debtors hold on for as long as they can, hoping that some other balance sheet in the system will prove to be the weakest link. The important point is that sooner or later asset prices come under pressure, not just the prices that were rising at 15 percent but all asset prices, and especially the price of the assets held by the most vulnerable debtors, who are forced to liquidate first.

When that happens, liquidity problems (the survival constraint) become solvency problems, and especially so for highly leveraged financial institutions. Even if they are not forced to sell assets in order to make promised payments, they may be forced to write down the valuation of those assets to reflect current market prices. For highly leveraged institutions, with financial liabilities many times larger than their capital base, it doesn't take much of a write-down to produce technical insolvency. And even before insolvency, asset write-downs can quickly generate serious liquidity problems as credit lines shrink to fit reduced collateral valuations. Liquidity and solvency problems thus reinforce one another on the way down, just as credit expansion and asset valuation do on the way up. This is the downside of the inherent instability of credit.

On the way up, as has been emphasized, the central bank tends not to have much traction, since borrowers and lenders share an interest in avoiding central bank discipline. On the way down a similar mutual interest, now in avoiding market discipline, brings both borrowers and lenders back to the central bank as the last available source of credit elasticity. "Lender of last resort" intervention involves the central bank extending credit when no one else will (or can); in effect, the central bank relaxes the survival constraint by providing current cash inflow to allow borrowers to delay the day of reckoning. Used wisely, such intervention can control the downturn and prevent it from turning into a rout. Used unwisely, such intervention can foster further continuation of unhealthy bubble conditions. In a crisis, as in normal times, the art of central banking is all about walking the fine line between providing too much discipline versus too much elasticity.

The Old Lombard Street

The impact and effectiveness of central bank control both depend crucially on the institutional organization of the banking system, and on its articulation with the financial system more generally. Walter Bagehot's *Lombard Street* explored these questions in the context of the London money market of his day, a set of institutional arrangements different in important respects from modern arrangements, but nonetheless a good starting point because the conclusions that Bagehot drew continue to shape the way we think today. The Bagehot principle that guided central bankers in the current crisis has its origin in that nineteenth-century book.

Today we summarize the Bagehot principle as "lend freely but at a high rate." Here are Bagehot's own words (1906 [1873], 197): "The end is to stay the panic. And for this purpose there are two rules:—First. That these loans should only be made at a very high rate of interest. . . . Secondly. That at this rate these advances should be made on all good banking securities, and as largely as the public ask for them." Why did Bagehot think this was wise policy for his world, and is it still wise policy for our own very different modern world?

Bagehot's world was based on a short-term commercial credit instrument known as the bill of exchange. Firms issued bills in order to buy inputs for their own production processes, and they accepted bills as payment for their own outputs. The bill of exchange was a promise to pay at a specific future date, perhaps in ninety days. For a fee, banks would "accept" bills, which meant guaranteeing payment. For another fee, banks would "discount" bills, which meant buying them for less than face value, the difference amounting to a rate of interest to be earned over the term to maturity. As payment for the bills, banks would offer either currency or a deposit account credit. Either way, the proceeds of the discount were most typically not held as idle balances but rather spent in payment of other maturing bills. In this way, the discount mechanism was crucial for British firms' management of their daily cash flow, in and out.

Ideally, over the ninety days between issue and maturity, the firm that issued the bill would use the inputs so acquired to produce output for sale, and then use the sale proceeds to pay the bill as it came due. Timely repayment thus depended on timely sale of the production financed by the bill. Assuming timely repayment, the banking business was all about managing one's portfolio of bills in order to match up the timing of cash inflows (from maturing bills) with the timing of cash outflows (for new discounts). If ever a firm failed to pay, however, then the accepting bank would experience a cash shortfall.

In this system, banks managed their own daily cash flow by managing the discount rate they quoted to their customers. If requests for discount were depleting one's cash reserve, one had merely to raise one's discount rate and the business would go elsewhere; if maturing bills were swelling one's cash reserve, one simply lowered the discount rate to attract additional interest-paying business. In this way, the market rate of interest fluctuated according to supply and demand. The rate of interest was high when requests for new discount were running ahead of repayments, and low when the balance went the other way.

It was in this institutional context that the Bank of England developed the principles of central bank management that laid the foundations for modern monetary theory. At first, so Bagehot relates, the Bank thought of itself as simply one among other banks, responsible to its shareholders for the profitability of its operations, and with no larger responsibility for the system as a whole. In accordance with this way of thinking, the Bank moved its discount rate in line with the market in order to attract its rightful share of the discount business.

The experience of periodic financial crises, however, eventually taught the lesson that the Bank was not like other banks insofar as it was the central repository of cash reserves for the entire system. In times of general crisis, all banks looked to the Bank of England for help, and in order to prepare for that day the Bank had to safeguard its own reserve. That meant keeping its own discount rate ordinarily somewhat higher than the market rate, even at the cost of sacrificing some discount business and thus shareholder profit.

In this context, the Bagehot principle can be understood as the distillation of hard-won practical wisdom about how to deal with a crisis when one comes. The proximate origin of the crisis could be many things, but from the point of view of the Bank it always took the form of a large, often sudden, demand for cash. Any hiccup in current sales would mean that maturing bills could not be paid by their issuer. As a consequence, the accepting bank would be called on to make good from its own resources, which involved drawing down reserves held at the Bank of England and then, should that prove insufficient, borrowing more.

If the Bank of England failed to lend in such a circumstance, the needy bank would be unable to meet its commitments and those who had been expecting payment from that bank would similarly find themselves unable to meet their own commitments, and so on and so on as the cascade of nonpayment spread throughout the economy. The Bagehot principle was designed to stop the potential cascade by providing completely elastic lending to needy banks against any security that would be acceptable in normal times. But it was also designed to provide discipline by charging a high rate of interest. Only those who really needed the cash would borrow at the high rate, and the high rate would also provide incentive to repay the loan as soon as possible.

The problem with elastic lending in time of crisis was that it tended to drain the note reserves of the Bank of England. Under the provisions of Peel's Act of 1844, the note issue was fixed, and any additional notes had to be backed 100 percent by additional gold reserves. In normal times, the Bank held a significant fraction of the note issue as reserve against deposits in the Banking Department, and it was these deposits that served as reserves for the banking system at large. During a crisis, the demand for cash was met both by paying out cash reserves (notes) and by expanding the supply of cash substitutes (deposits). When the crisis was over, the emergency loans would be repaid, the emergency supply of cash substitutes would be extinguished, and the Bank's cash reserve would be built up again. That is how it was supposed to work, and how in fact it did work, so long as the crisis remained within the confines of Britain itself.

The policy of elastic lending ran into trouble, however, whenever the crisis assumed international dimensions, which more often than not it did, given the centrality of the pound sterling in the world trading system. The same bills of exchange apparatus that merchants used to finance domestic production was used also to finance foreign trade, trade not only between British merchants and their foreign counterparties but also between different foreign parties themselves. No matter where you were in the world, if you wanted to import goods, you were likely to pay by issuing a bill of exchange payable at some London bank and your counterparty was likely to present that bill of exchange for discount prior to maturity in order to raise cash to meet his own payment obligations.

The problem was that foreigners did not consider either notes or deposits to be acceptable means of payment; they wanted gold. (Mechanically, payment would be demanded in notes, and those notes would be presented to the Issue Department at the Bank of England for payment in gold.) The effect of a foreign demand for cash was thus to reduce the supply of currency in Britain and also, more important, to drain the Bank's holding of gold, which served as reserve for the nation as a whole.

Not only firms and banks but also nations have to look after their daily balance of cash inflows and outflows, and for nations on the gold standard that meant the daily balance of gold flows. For Britain, gold flows were mostly about the balance between payments on maturing international bills of exchange (gold inflows) versus requests for new discounts (gold outflows). The money rate of interest in London was thus a symptom of international as well as domestic balance and imbalance, and the central position of the Bank of England in the London money market meant that its reserve was essentially the international as well as the national reserve. In normal times, if gold was flowing out of Britain, the Bank raised its discount rate in order to make new discounts less attractive, thus shifting the balance of payments back in its favor. The high rate of interest recommended by Bagehot for times of crisis was intended not only to limit the supply of funds to those most in need, but also to safeguard the nation's gold reserve in the face of a potential external drain.

By 1873, when Bagehot was writing, the Bank had gotten used to its role as lender of last resort *domestically*, and this was the main focus of the Bagehot principle. But the Bank had not at all gotten used to its role as lender of last resort *internationally*, nor did Bagehot endorse such a role. For him, elasticity was all about *domestic* lending—here the Bank should not safeguard its reserve but rather mobilize it, down to the last farthing. But once those farthings come into the hands of foreigners who ask gold for them, the Bank has to stop. It can create more deposits to meet an internal drain, but it cannot create more gold to meet an external drain. In a crisis, the Bank could and did suspend the gold reserve requirement for notes, thus freeing up its gold holdings for payment to foreigners. But if that buffer was ever exhausted, there would be no choice but to suspend convertibility.

Clearly, the ideal solution would be to get foreigners to behave like domestic residents, which is to say to accept sterling balances (deposits or securities) as substitutes for gold. Britain's most significant colonial possession already did so, as the young John Maynard Keynes pointed out in his first book, *Indian Currency and Finance* (1913). According to Keynes, the case of India showed that a gold-sterling exchange system was a workable arrangement for international monetary affairs more generally. But World War I, the Great Depression, and World War II dashed that dream. What we got instead, after the dust cleared, was a gold-dollar exchange system established at Bretton Woods in 1944, which became a plain dollar standard in 1973 after the United States abandoned gold convertibility.

The New Lombard Street

Our modern world is not Bagehot's world, and not only because the dollar and the Federal Reserve have replaced the pound and the Bank of England, and the dollar standard has replaced the gold standard. For us, the most important money market instrument is not the bill of exchange but rather something called a "repurchase agreement," or repo. Repos are issued not to finance the progress of real goods toward final sale, as in Bagehot's world, but rather to finance the holding of some financial asset.

Formally, the underlying financial asset serves as collateral for a short-term loan, often as short as overnight. The "repurchase" refers to a legal construction whereby the short-term loan is arranged as the sale of an asset combined with an agreement to repurchase the asset at the original sale price plus some rate of interest. The original sale price is lower than the market value of the asset by an amount known as the "haircut"; the purpose of the haircut is to provide extra collateral for the loan, so the size of the haircut varies with the perceived riskiness of the asset being used for collateral. The lowest repo rates, and the lowest haircuts, apply when the collateral for the loan is a Treasury bill.

In our world, the Treasury repo market plays a special role as the main interface between the money market and the Fed. (I speak here of the way things worked before the crisis.) The Fed enters that market typically as a lender, offering short-term loans of high-powered money (deposits at the Fed) in return for Treasury bill collateral. On a daily basis, the Fed might "tighten money" by allowing outstanding repo loans to mature without replacement, or it might "loosen money" by offering new and larger loans. The immediate counterparties to these loans are the "primary dealers," so called for their commitment to bid for Treasury securities whenever the Treasury wishes to borrow. In normal times, the funds that the dealers borrow from the Fed at the daily repo auction are a low-cost source of finance for their main business of making two-way markets in Treasury securities by posting offers to buy and sell.

The special position of the primary dealers can be considered a legacy of World War II, when the U.S. government issued vast volumes of Treasury securities not only to finance its own war effort but also to finance the war spending of its allies. When the war was over, the war debt remained, on the balance sheets of households that would use it to purchase houses and cars, on the balance sheets of corporations that would use it to fund conversion from wartime production, and on the balance sheets of banks that would use it to fund private loans. All of these debt holders depended on the ability to convert government debt readily into spendable cash, which is to say on the existence of the two-way markets provided by security dealers.

During the war and its immediate aftermath, the Fed directly fixed the price of government debt, and directly backstopped the convertibility of government debt into cash at that fixed price. After the Fed-Treasury Accord of 1951, the Fed no longer fixed the price of Treasury securities but it did continue to provide liquidity support to the Treasury market. Eventually, even that responsibility passed on to the primary dealers, with the Fed backing up the dealers by providing liquidity support to them through its daily operations in Treasury repo.

Here then is how the New Lombard Street works. Whereas Bagehot's central bank used the discount rate to manage the system, the Fed focuses its attention on the price of overnight lending in the federal funds market, which is an interbank market for deposits at the Fed. (An overnight federal funds loan involves receipt of reserve funds today in return for payment of reserve funds tomorrow.) The Fed does not directly lend or borrow in the federal funds market, so the "effective" federal funds rate fluctuates depending on supply and demand. Instead the Fed uses the Treasury repo market to control the supply of the underlying deposits that are borrowed and lent in the federal funds market.

The Fed's monopoly supply of bank reserves gives it considerable control over the federal funds market, but there is quite a bit of slippage between conditions in the federal funds market and funding liquidity more generally. The Fed is only a small player in the enormous general collateral repo market where security dealers fund most of their activity. And it is not a player at all in the offshore market in Eurodollar bank deposits, which is always available to banks as an alternative to federal funds and, indeed, has grown up to be the most liquid money market in the world. In both repo and Eurodollar markets, borrowers and lenders find one another and do business outside the reach of the Fed.[5] As always, private credit elasticity is a substitute for public credit elasticity, indeed often an attractive substitute.

Nevertheless, it remains true that balance sheet operations by the Fed affect funding liquidity, and thus also market liquidity, through the risk calculus of security dealers. Dealers post prices at which they are willing to buy and sell a particular security—the buy (bid) price lower than the sell (offer or ask) price—and then they adjust those prices depending on customer response. If they find themselves accumulating a large position in a particular security, they lower their posted prices. The main idea behind this practice is to control risk by allowing their exposure to increase only if it comes at an attractive price. But the effect of lowering price is also to control cash flow by attracting more buyers and fewer sellers, hence more cash inflow through net sales and less cash outflow through net purchases.

Actual dealing operations are more sophisticated than this, but even this simple account is enough to make clear that security dealers provide a sensitive link between conditions in the money market and conditions in broader financial markets. At one end of the chain of causation, we have the Fed setting the federal funds rate; at the other end, we have private dealers seeking profit by making markets. Private dealers borrow in the money market in order to finance their market-making operations in capital markets; that is the way that "funding liquidity" in money markets gets translated into "market liquidity" in capital markets.[6] The market for Treasury securities is the first place this market liquidity shows up, but then it gets spread by means of arbitrage more or less quickly and efficiently to other related markets such as those for corporate bonds and, more recently, residential mortgage-backed securities. (I remind the reader again that I speak of the way things worked before the crisis.)

By contrast to Bagehot's time, under modern conditions the Fed's discount window has fallen into disuse. When individual banks need money to meet their commitments at the daily clearing, they usually raise it from other banks in the wholesale money market. And when the banking system as a whole needs money, that money is usually raised by selling security holdings into liquid markets. Both channels are backstopped ultimately by the Fed's commitment to stabilize the federal funds rate around a chosen target, and by its intervention to make good on that commitment by lending in the Treasury repo market. Put starkly, under modern conditions the Fed is *always* lending freely, but only to primary security dealers, only against Treasury security collateral, and only at the Treasury repo rate that corresponds to the target federal funds rate.

This practice was supposed to prevent crisis. The way it was supposed to work is that the Fed would lend freely to the dealers, and arbitrage would do the rest, modulo some term spread between Treasury bills and longer-maturity issues, and some credit spread between Treasuries and nongovernment issues. By raising the federal funds rate, the Fed would raise the funding cost of making markets and thus induce some deleveraging and push around the spreads. By loosening, the Fed would lower the funding cost and thus lessen the pressure to liquidate, again pushing around the spreads. That is how it was supposed to work and, in fact, how it did work until the recent crisis.

In the crisis, this system broke down. As asset valuations came into question, haircuts for secured borrowing rose sharply, even for Treasuries but especially for non-Treasury securities, and the result was forced deleveraging and disordered markets.[7] The problem was that, in private credit markets, collateral is marked to market, not to fundamental value. Bagehot's admonition to lend freely against any security that would be acceptable collateral in normal times is a principle for central banks only. Individual banks have always followed the save-yourself rule of lending only against securities that can be readily liquidated in current extraordinary times. This time was no exception.

In response to the severe contraction in private liquidity, the Fed stepped in, widening the category of counterparties to which it was prepared to lend, and widening also the category of collateral it was prepared to accept. Borrowers and lenders who had previously found each other in the wholesale money market now found each other only through the intermediation of the Fed. The result was, first, a hollowing out of the Fed's balance sheet as it sold off its Treasury securities (to the former lenders) to fund new loans (to the former borrowers), and then an explosion of the Fed's balance sheet as it expanded its deposit liabilities (to the former lenders), and used the proceeds to fund additional lending (to the former borrowers).

The Fed's response to the crisis can be understood as a modern adaptation of the Bagehot principle, at least in part. Rephrased in terms that connect up with modern institutional arrangements, Bagehot can be understood as arguing that the central bank should act as money market *dealer* of last resort, providing both borrowers and lenders with what they want but at prices that are worse than they would be getting if they were meeting directly rather than on the balance sheet of the Bank. In line with Bagehot's conception, not only would the borrower pay a high borrowing rate, but also the lender would accept a low deposit rate. It is the gap between the borrowing and lending rates that provides incentive for borrowers and lenders to find one another again once the storm dies down. In effect, the Bagehot principle can be understood as recommending that the central bank post a wide bid-ask spread in the money market and use its balance sheet to absorb the resulting flow of orders.

That is more or less exactly what the Fed did in the various emergency liquidity facilities that it opened in response to the crisis. The Fed's bid-ask spread was not always as wide as Bagehot might have wished—the Fed charged only a small spread over the federal funds target for its Term Auction Facility (TAF) lending facility, and it also paid interest on its deposit liabilities. But other facilities had wider spreads, and as a consequence wound down rather quickly—to wit, the commercial paper funding facility and the central bank swap facility. So far, so Bagehot.

What was not Bagehot was the *level* of interest rates, which fell almost to zero. This was possible only because the Fed, unlike the nineteenth-century Bank of England, faces no reserve constraint in terms of gold. The whole world treats dollar deposits at the Fed not only as good as dollar currency, but also as the ultimate world reserve in a time of crisis. That means that the Fed, unlike the Bank of England, can create both more domestic dollars to meet an internal drain *and* more international dollars to meet an external drain. The Fed has no need to safeguard its holding of world reserves by keeping the federal funds rate high, since world reserves are its own liability.

But just because the Fed *can* evade the reserve constraint that others must obey does not mean that it *should*. There are reasons to question whether such evasion is the correct policy even for crisis times, and a fortiori for normal times. From a Hawtreyan point of view, the very fact of the crisis stands as an indictment of Fed policy in the years leading up to it. Hawtrey would have had no trouble understanding the present crisis as a consequence of the central bank losing control of a runaway credit expansion; at root the boom must be a problem of excessive elasticity and insufficient discipline. How did it happen that the inherent instability of credit was allowed to play itself out as it did? Where was the Fed?

TWO

Origins of the Present System

Monetary thought arises from monetary experience, but with a long and variable lag. In 1913, the Federal Reserve Act established a central bank in the United States, but it could not at the same time establish any new tradition of monetary thought. There was also no American Hawtrey on hand to help out, for the simple reason that there had been no American central bank since the charter of the Second Bank of the United States had been allowed to expire in 1836. At the origin of the modern monetary system, institutional change was dramatic and rapid, but older patterns of thought continued to organize public and professional discourse.

From National Banking to the Fed

In 1913, what Americans knew was not central banking but rather the National Banking System, an artifact of Civil War finance. The National Currency Act of 1863 and the National Banking Act of 1864 had created the national bank note, which was issued by private banks against collateral of a special issue of government bonds paying 2 percent interest. The main purpose of the act was to support the market for government bonds, but the long-run consequence was to fix the supply of note currency. Even after return to the gold standard in 1879, this quantitative constraint on the national bank note issue remained. It is because of this fixed note supply that the National Banking System can be said to have been founded on the "currency principle," which understands bank note currency as analogous to government-issued fiat currency; such a currency is supposed to retain its value only because it is kept scarce.

On top of the inelastic note currency there was a potentially elastic deposit currency, founded on the "banking principle," which anchors the value of deposit currency by means of ready convertibility into the better note currency (or gold). Prevailing banking theory, variously called the commercial loan theory or the real bills doctrine, suggested that individual banks were on safe ground, with respect to maintaining all-important convertibility, so long as they confined their asset holdings to "self-liquidating" short-term commercial loans. The idea was that the scheduled loan repayments would provide a ready mechanism for repayment of deposits, and hence for contraction of the deposit currency, should the public so desire. This mechanism was supposed to work not only for individual banks but also for the banking system as a whole. So long as bank assets were limited largely to commercial loans, the supply of credit and money was supposed automatically to expand and contract in line with the "needs of trade." No central authority was supposed to be required; automatic self-regulation would make active management unnecessary.

That is how the National Banking System was supposed to work, but not in fact how it did work. In the U.S. context, the most significant fluctuation in the needs of trade was seasonal, a consequence of the largely agricultural character of the country at the time. The inelasticity of the note issue, combined with the rigidity of required reserve ratios, meant that deposits could not so easily expand and contract as needed. An individual lending bank soon found itself losing reserves as newly created deposits were transferred as payment to banks elsewhere in the system, and therefore found itself forced to borrow its reserves back. At harvest time, when credit was expanding generally, other banks would also be attempting to obtain the same reserves, thus driving up the wholesale money rate of interest. Anticipating the difficulty of acquiring reserves in time of need, banks therefore held on to excess reserves in time of slack, sending them to the New York money market where they drove down the wholesale money rate of interest.

Reserves were thus always either too tight, pushing up interest rates and attracting gold inflows from the more elastic international money market, or they were too loose, providing cheap funds for stock market speculation in New York. The result was a regular seasonality in interest rates, punctuated by regular financial crises in 1873, 1884, 1893, and finally 1907. In each of these crises, bankers found a way to get around the acute reserve scarcity by issuing quasi-legal temporary emergency currency against private debt collateral. The Aldrich-Vreeland Act of 1908 created for the first time a legal framework for this emergency procedure. And then, following the abortive 1912 Aldrich Bill, the Federal Reserve Act of 1913 went even further.[1]

For the framers of the Federal Reserve Act, the problem with the National Banking System seemed clear. Deposits were not appropriately elastic because reserves were not appropriately elastic, and reserves were not appropriately elastic because the note issue was not appropriately elastic. The Federal Reserve Act sought to address all three problems at the same time, and thus to address not only the problem of occasional emergency but also the problem of regular seasonal stress. To make the supply of reserves elastic, the act created Federal Reserve Banks charged with discounting commercial loans, to add reserves to the system. And to make the supply of notes elastic, the act provided for (elastic) commercial loans to replace (inelastic) government bonds as collateral backing for the note issue. As one observer remarked, "Taking the system as a whole, it will be seen that it gives a thoroughly elastic supply of credit. It has all of the necessary elements: elastic note issue, elastic deposits and elastic reserves."[2]

The Federal Reserve System was thus founded on the idea that the commercial loan theory for individual banks could be extended to a theory of central banking as well. Gold convertibility would safeguard the value of the new Federal Reserve note, and individual Reserve Banks would be on safe ground in expanding their deposit liabilities so long as the corresponding assets were limited to self-liquidating short-term commercial loans. Since the Reserve Banks were in fact banks, this extension of standard theory probably did not seem very far-fetched.

A more controversial extension was the inclusion of business and farming loans, in addition to the more orthodox trade acceptances (the classic bills of exchange), as eligible collateral.[3] Even trade acceptances had already proven not to be dependably self-liquidating in a crisis—hence the need for a central bank lender of last resort—so the expansion to even less clearly self-liquidating paper constituted an important move away from the fundamental principle underlying the commercial loan theory. But that move had long before been effected as an adaptation of British institutions to American conditions.[4] The plain fact of the matter was that industry and farming were relatively much more important for the U.S. economy than for the British, so the idea of focusing banking narrowly around trade never had much plausibility in the United States, especially for banks located in the industrial or agricultural heartland.

Notwithstanding this important nod to indigenous conditions, the commercial loan theory continued to exert its intellectual force in the framers' attempt to draw a line between productive and speculative credit, the former being eligible and the latter ineligible for discount at the Fed. By insisting on this distinction, the framers were willfully ignoring a further indigenous development, in fact trying to legislate that indigenous development out of existence. Unlike their British counterparts, and notwithstanding orthodox banking theory, American banks had always been more or less deeply involved with financing not only working capital but also fixed capital. As a consequence, most banks had substantial holdings of bonds and stocks, loans on bond and stock collateral, and loans on mortgage or real estate collateral, all assets that orthodox banking theory would relegate to savings banks or other long-term investors.

Because of this asset structure, American banks had come to rely for their daily liquidity not so much on the self-liquidating character of their commercial loan portfolios but rather on the "shiftability" of their investment portfolios in liquid markets. Lines of credit with other banks typically served as the first line of defense. But after that, high-quality bonds were used as a secondary reserve, either by selling them outright or by using them as collateral to obtain funds by borrowing (repurchase agreements). Such shiftability depended ultimately on security dealers and other speculators being willing to buy the assets that banks wanted to sell, and so-called speculative credit was always the lifeblood of the dealer business. Thus, paradoxically, it was speculative credit, not productive credit, that had been the source of liquidity for most American banks in the years before the Fed. The framers knew this, but they viewed it as part of the problem that they were trying to fix.

In the event, and notwithstanding the framers' best legislative efforts, the act did not succeed in replacing the indigenous system of "artificial" liquidity with an idealized system of "natural" liquidity. Rather the act merely made clear that one particular subset of assets, commercial loans, would be shiftable to the Fed in time of crisis, and not the rest of the assets that the banks had been more commonly using among themselves. But there was nothing in the act to prevent banks from continuing their former practice, and so they did, after the founding of the Fed, just as before; as one observer summarized in 1918, "Liquidity is tantamount to shiftability."[5]

The problem would come not in normal times, but in times of crisis. Predictably, the shiftability of even high-quality bonds would prove unreliable when everyone was trying to sell and there were no buyers. In this regard, the supposed "artificial" liquidity of shiftable assets was no different from the supposed "natural" liquidity of commercial loans. In a crisis, liquidity *always* depends on interbank accommodation. "It rests upon the ability either to draw upon unused reservoirs of reserves [such as the international gold reserve] or to create new forms of reserve money [such as quasi-legal clearinghouse notes] that can be used as a basis for an expansion of loans."[6]

From this point of view, the most important innovation of the Federal Reserve System was to provide a routine mechanism for creation of reserve money in times of crisis. "Under the Federal Reserve System it is of course apparent that liquidity is a question of shiftability to the Federal Reserve banks."[7] At the time the act was written, the commercial loan theory of banking was in the mind of its framers, so they favored limiting shiftability to the normally self-liquidating commercial loan. The fatal implication of this limitation would not become evident until the banking crisis that followed the stock market crash of October 1929.

Meanwhile, from the very start it was clear to observers that the system was not working as the framers had intended. Requests for discount accommodation by member banks were never very strong, so, in an attempt to acquire some earning assets, the Reserve Banks found themselves buying eligible paper in the open market, which is to say from dealers in that paper rather than from banks. Furthermore, in an attempt to fulfill their remit to replace the National Bank note with the Federal Reserve note, the Reserve Banks found themselves entering the bond market to purchase the underlying 2 percent bonds.[8] In these operations we find the origin of subsequent so-called open market operations, which can be understood in retrospect as the Fed's operational recognition of the centrality of shiftability, notwithstanding the language of the act. Practice was proving different from theory.

Had events not intervened, the Fed might have continued to evolve organically by developing explicit mechanisms to support the indigenous shiftability mechanism, so providing a liquidity backstop for security markets as a way of supporting the liquidity of banks that relied on the shiftability of their assets in those markets. The ideology of the commercial loan theory stood in the way, of course, but would have bowed to reality in this as in prior adaptations. In an alternative counterfactual history, the Fed might thus have eventually got around to developing a lending facility for security dealers, long before the collapse of Bear Stearns in March 2008 forced it to open the Primary Dealer Credit Facility. And it might also have eventually got around to developing a policy for accepting investment assets, maybe even including mortgages backed by real estate, well before the collapse of Lehman Brothers in September 2008 forced it to extend discount eligibility to any investment-grade security. In other words, the Fed might have been able to use its facilities to shape market developments ex ante, rather than waiting to mop up the mess ex post.

Such a natural process of institutional evolution was, however, diverted by the cosmic catastrophes of World War I, the worldwide Depression, and World War II. From a banking perspective, the significant consequence of these events was an explosion of government debt and an ongoing responsibility of the new Federal Reserve System to ensure liquid markets for that debt. By cosmic accident, and quite against the intentions of both the orthodox framers of the 1913 act and their shiftability opponents, Treasury debt, *not* commercial loans, thus became the shiftable asset sine qua non, and the consequent liquidity of Treasury markets became the source of liquidity for the entire system.

From War Finance to Catastrophe

In preparation for U.S. entry into World War I, the Federal Reserve Act was amended on September 7, 1916, to permit Federal Reserve notes to be issued against Treasury security collateral. In this way, hardly was the ink dry on the Act before the founding principle that notes could safely be issued only against self-liquidating commercial loans was simply shunted aside. (For the sake of appearances, eligible note collateral was extended not to the securities themselves but only to Reserve Bank loans against government security collateral, but that was a distinction without a difference.) Not only that, but Reserve Bank loans against government security collateral were subsequently pegged at a preferential rate, below the commercial rate and below even the yield on the security itself.

Conservative bankers thus saw their worst nightmare realized, that the government would use its authority over the monetary apparatus to gain an advantage over private borrowers. On the other hand, the very same bankers were quick to take advantage of the arbitrage involved in borrowing at the discount window to invest in government securities. Federal debt expanded from about $1 billion in 1917 to $25 billion in 1919, with the Federal Reserve System itself absorbing about $2 billion and acting as fiscal agent to distribute much of the rest.[9] In effect, the Fed acted as the government's prime dealer in the Treasury market, absorbing excess issue into its own inventory and financing that inventory by expanding its own monetary liabilities.

During the war, the Fed acted both to maintain liquidity in the Treasury bond market and to put a floor under the price of the bonds so that the Treasury could continue to borrow cheaply. After the war, the price floor was relaxed and the discount rate was raised, but the practice of liquidity support continued. The vaunted elasticity of deposits, notes, and reserves in the postwar Federal Reserve System thus derived from their two-way exchangeability for Treasury debt, *not* from the self-liquidating properties of commercial loans. Indeed, despite the privileged position given to commercial loans by the Federal Reserve Act, the relative importance of such loans continued to decline throughout the 1920s in favor of investments in bonds and mortgages secured by real estate. Shiftability thus continued to be the true source of liquidity in the system, after the war as before. The difference was that the dependence on speculative credit was less visible, as Treasury securities and repurchase agreements using Treasury collateral became the principal secondary reserve, and as the Fed rather than private security dealers stood as the ultimate guarantor of shiftability.

This involvement of the Fed in what would formerly have been considered speculative credit is probably one reason that, at the New York Fed anyway, attention shifted away from "qualitative" control of credit (limiting credit to productive use) and toward "quantitative" control, specifically discount rate policy directed at affecting the price of credit.[10] This shift of focus involved an additional step away from banking orthodoxy, which abhorred active management, but was very much in line with developments in British central banking theory since Bagehot, to wit, the writings of Hawtrey, which strongly influenced Benjamin Strong, the president of the New York Fed.[11] Indeed, the so-called Strong rule can be understood in this context as establishing a benchmark against which more activist intervention could be calibrated.[12]

The Strong rule involved setting the discount rate slightly above the market rate of interest and then using open market operations in Treasury securities to control the quantity of discounts.[13] The idea was that, as credit expanded, demand for discounts would rise, but expansionary open market operations would meet that demand shift without requiring the actual volume of discounts to rise. Then, as credit contracted, demand for discounts would contract, but contractionary open market operations would meet that demand shift also without requiring the actual volume of discounts to fall. The idea of the Strong rule was thus to use discretionary open market operations to achieve the idealized result that the commercial loan theory imagined could be automatic. In the new Federal Reserve System operating under the Strong rule, reserves could expand as needed and contract when no longer needed, but this result was achieved by active trading in existing government debt rather than by passive discounting of newly created commercial loans.

The most immediate application of the Strong rule was to the seasonal fluctuation of the system. Here the rule was used to achieve an approximate neutrality across the annual cycle by expanding temporarily and then contracting back again. Indeed, to signal its intention of neutrality, the Fed engaged in repurchase agreements with security dealers, buying assets when seasonal credit needs expanded but at the same time agreeing to sell them back at a future date when the seasonal need was expected to recede. Note that when the Fed does repo with a security dealer, it lends money to that dealer and accepts Treasury collateral in return. This is exactly the kind of speculative lending that orthodox banking theory abhorred, but the effect was to expand reserves in order to enable banks to engage in exactly the kind of productive lending that orthodox banking theory celebrated! As always, it is not so easy to separate productive from speculative credit.

Having conquered the seasonal (farming) problem, the question arose whether the Fed might also be able to do something about the cyclical (industrial) problem. Here, instead of a neutral policy, one might conceive a countercyclical policy along Hawtreyan lines that attempts some constraint during a credit expansion in order to head off an unsustainable speculative upswing, and some ease during a credit contraction in order to head off a downward spiral of liquidation. When it desired to restrain credit, the Fed would sell assets until the quantity of discounts rose, and this unusually high volume of discounts was supposed to exert a restraining influence on bank lending. When it desired to loosen credit, the Fed would buy assets until the quantity of discounts fell, and this unusually low volume of discounts was supposed to exert an encouraging influence. This is the kind of thing that Benjamin Strong was experimenting with at the New York Fed in the 1920s, and it seemed to help temper cyclical downturns in 1924 and 1927.

All of this domestic smoothing, both seasonal and cyclical, took place within the context of attempts at the international level to put back in place some version of the prewar gold standard. Indeed, for some people, the whole point of the Federal Reserve System was to keep domestic seasonal and cyclical fluctuations inside the country, and thus prevent them from disturbing the global gold market.[14] When additional domestic bank reserves were needed, the Fed was to provide them itself, and when they were no longer needed, the Fed was to reabsorb them. As a consequence, the world would be better off, but so would the United States because its domestic interest rates could be both less volatile and lower on average. Why so? There would be no need to compensate foreigners in the gold market for a seasonal round-trip journey into the dollar and out again. And also, in the event of cyclical crises, there would be no need to spike rates to attract emergency gold reserves since all of the needed emergency currency could be created by the Fed.

This international perspective helps to explain the Fed's policy throughout the 1920s of keeping interest rates low and stable while sterilizing temporary gold flows both in and out. This policy has often been interpreted as an attempt to help the rest of the world, and especially England, to return to the gold standard.[15] But the Fed could quite reasonably have believed that it was setting rates where they naturally would be, now that the United States was no longer reliant on the international gold market to meet fluctuating reserve demand. In retrospect, however, we recognize that this policy was the fuel that fired the stock market bubble that led to the crash in October 1929. Inadvertently, Strong's interest rate policy proved to be the original stock market put.

By the time the Fed realized what was happening, however, it was too late. Contractionary open market operations in 1928 and 1929 proved insufficient to halt the boom, as credit outside the banking system continued to expand on the basis of expanding asset valuations. At the peak of the speculative boom, the New York banks served as little more than brokers, using their "brokers' loans for the account of others" to channel funds to the stock market despite efforts of the Federal Reserve to stem the flow. Here is the original "shadow banking system." In this context, the Fed's attempts to halt expansion by raising the discount rate came too late to be effectual, as rising interest rates merely attracted more funds to the market, even while threatening the capital values on which so much bank lending was based. In the last stage of the boom, high U.S. interest rates even attracted funds from abroad, thus reversing the credit flows that had sustained the postwar pattern of international payment commitments.

Once the collapse began, expansionary open market operations proved insufficient to halt it. Focused as the Fed was on the discount of commercial loans, it was prepared to lend freely in a crisis, but *not* against the private securities whose falling value was undermining the solvency of member banks.[16] Shiftability of those assets thus proved to be a fair-weather friend, just as advocates had anticipated. What those advocates did not anticipate, however, was the inherent instability of credit, to wit, the way fair-weather shiftability would operate to inflate asset valuations on the way up, and the way the subsequent freeze would operate to deflate asset valuations on the way down. And nobody anticipated how the collapse of the shadow banking system, which was outside the Fed's control, would undermine the actual banking system, which was supposed to be under the Fed's care.

The important point, for our story, is that under American conditions, the money market and the securities markets have *always* been completely intertwined and, as a consequence, it has *never* been possible to distinguish speculative from productive credit. This intertwining predates the Fed, having its origins in bank reliance on shiftability under the National Banking System. What was new with the Fed was the emphasis on the commercial loan (in the enabling legislation) and then on government debt (as a consequence of war), but the intertwining of money and securities markets remained. Intervention to stabilize seasonal and cyclical fluctuations produced low and stable money rates of interest, which supported the investment boom that fueled the Roaring Twenties but also produced an unsustainable asset price bubble.

Just as easy money helped to inflate the securities bubble, so too did the bursting bubble operate to implode the monetary system. As the banking system collapsed in a series of crises from 1931 to 1933, so too did the money supply. Following Friedman and Schwartz, modern economists criticize the Fed for allowing this, indeed for exacerbating deflation by the ill-considered idea to raise discount rates in 1931 in order to stem gold outflow.[17] At the time, the economist Irving Fisher made a similar argument, emphasizing how falling prices had exacerbated the problem of over-indebtedness and thus turned a business downturn into a business depression.[18] Writing in 1933, Fisher anticipated that President Roosevelt's efforts to reflate would quickly restore the precrisis price level, thus turning a depression back into a more normal recession—but that didn't happen. Devaluation of the dollar against gold did not produce similar devaluation of the dollar against commodities, and subsequent vigorous monetary expansion was largely absorbed in expanding bank reserves.

In retrospect, the Fed certainly could have started its monetary expansion earlier and proceeded more aggressively, and it could have promptly suspended gold convertibility in 1931 rather than raising the discount rate. But unless the Fed was prepared to discount the private securities that made up the bulk of bank balance sheets, the banks would have failed anyway. Milton Friedman blamed the ideology of the commercial loan theory for distracting the Fed from the collapsing money supply. Perhaps more important, the ideology of the commercial loan theory prevented the Fed from monetizing bank assets during a crisis because the Fed considered these assets to be inappropriately speculative.

Noncommercial Credit in Depression and War

As the banking system collapsed, so too did the fragile intellectual balancing act between conservative banking and the shiftability view that had been supporting the Fed's cautious experimentation throughout the 1920s. Most pressing, defaults on bank deposit liabilities posed again the question of what is an appropriate bank asset, since bank insolvency was mainly a problem of falling market value of asset holdings and of defaults on long-term lending. Some saw an opportunity to reassert the shaping idea of the original Federal Reserve Act that self-liquidating commercial loans are the only appropriate assets for an institution that issues deposit liabilities that can be withdrawn on demand. Others, looking even further back in history, argued that deposit liabilities should be matched not with credit of even the very best kind, but only with monetary reserves, thus achieving "100 percent reserve" money.[19]

The Banking Act of 1933, often referred to as the Glass-Steagall Act, came down on neither side of this debate. Instead, it merely required separation of commercial and investment banking activities into distinct corporate entities, a measure that mainly affected large New York banks such as J. P. Morgan and left the asset portfolios of other banks largely untouched. Crucially, protection of bank deposits was achieved not by regulation of bank assets but rather by the addition of deposit insurance through the newly established Federal Deposit Insurance Corporation.

Subsequently, the Banking Act of 1935, introduced by the Utah banker Marriner S. Eccles after his November 1934 appointment as chairman of the Federal Reserve Board, gave the Fed the power to discount any "sound" asset, not just commercial loans. The effect, as one observer later pointed out, was to eliminate any distinction between liquidity and solvency. "Immediate liquidity is simply 'rediscountability' and long run liquidity is identical with solvency."[20] Even more, the effect was to make liquidity into a matter of government policy, not commercial calculation. "But it now appears that institutional, legal, or conventional liquidity, in the form of rediscountability or convertibility[,] is the only feasible arrangement."[21]

This radical redefinition of liquidity as being entirely a matter of Fed policy followed naturally from the prior radical redefinition of solvency as being entirely a matter of the policy of the Reconstruction Finance Corporation (established 1932), the Federal Home Loan Bank Board (1932), or the Federal Deposit Insurance Corporation (1933). If the government said you were solvent then you were, because that meant the government would stand behind you and prop you up with guarantees and loans. The government did not buy outright the troubled assets that were weighing down bank balance sheets; rather it recapitalized the surviving banks in order to give them time to work their way out of trouble.

In retrospect, the Banking Act of 1935 represents the final triumph of the shiftability view and the final repudiation of the commercial loan theory.[22] By committing itself to lend against any sound asset, in effect the government committed to making all sound assets equally and fully liquid. This commitment would have far-reaching consequences once the emergency was over, but at the time no one was thinking about that. Indeed, the radical nature of the shift went largely unnoticed among all the other radical measures being proposed, attempted, and abandoned in the chaotic experimentation that was the New Deal. Meanwhile, the failure of even very aggressive monetary expansion to produce recovery had led to discredit of monetary theories across the board, so policy attention turned elsewhere, specifically to direct government spending.

Government spending had long been a part of the policy response to the Great Depression, but largely for the purpose of relief. Then, in 1936, the British economist John Maynard Keynes published his *General Theory of Employment, Interest, and Money*, arguing that spending could also produce recovery.[23] Writing in 1938, the Harvard economist Alvin Hansen proposed an adaptation of the Keynesian idea for American conditions: "Governments all over the world are in the process of becoming intermediaries between the ultimate savers and investment outlets, but the process of production is still carried on by private enterprise. This is neither socialism in production nor even in the ownership of wealth. The government is becoming an investment banker."[24]

In the event, it was not the government-financed investment boom envisioned by Hansen but rather World War II that finally produced sufficient spending to bring about full employment, as well as an essentially planned economy in which production for war priorities drove all investment and credit allocation decisions. In wartime, even more than in depression, solvency and liquidity were a matter of government policy, not commercial calculation. Throughout the war, the interest rate on Treasury debt was fixed at 3/8 percent for three-month bills and between 2 and 2½ percent for long-term bonds, and it was the job of the Fed to support these prices by offering two-way convertibility into cash. As in World War I, government debt exploded (from $48 billion to $235 billion) and so did Federal Reserve credit (from $2 billion to $22 billion).[25]

War, depression, and then war again thus finally expunged memory of the National Banking System, as well as any very clear memory of the commercial loan theory as an alternative to the shiftability concept. By the end of World War II, banking and credit had been a matter of government control for an entire generation, and that itself explains why wartime controls remained in effect so long. Within the Fed, especially within the New York Fed under Allan Sproul, there was some institutional memory of how things used to be. But it was not until the Fed-Treasury Accord of March 1951 that the Fed was released from its wartime responsibility to peg the price of government debt.

Subsequently, under the "bills only" policy of the new board chairman William McChesney Martin, the Fed was also released from ongoing responsibility to directly manage the market in long-term debt.[26] Thenceforth, the shiftability of long-maturity Treasury bonds would depend on private security dealers, who funded themselves in the short-term money market. The Fed, operating through the Treasury bill market, would support shiftability in the securities market only indirectly, by supporting the funding liquidity of the dealers. In this way, starting with the market for Treasury securities, the pre-Depression (and pre-Fed) intertwining of the money market with the securities market was put back in place after World War II.

THREE

The Age of Management

The triumph of the shiftability view in the 1935 Bank Act meant that, from then on, the Fed was prepared to act fully as lender of last resort, accepting as collateral any "sound" asset and not limiting itself to short-term self-liquidating paper. Two years later, in a communication by the Federal Open Market Committee (FOMC) issued in April 1937, the Fed went even further, committing itself to maintaining "orderly conditions in the money market" quite generally.[1] What this meant was that, instead of waiting passively for banks to request loans, the Fed was prepared to intervene proactively by buying and selling securities in the open market. In 1935, shiftability was supposed to be provided by private dealers, operating with the knowledge that the Fed's discount window would be available to them if they got into trouble. That wasn't enough, so in 1937 the Fed took over responsibility for providing shiftability itself. In effect, the Fed committed itself to act as a security dealer.

In retrospect, this 1937 commitment represents a very significant step, since it brought to the forefront of policy consideration the whole question of capital asset pricing. After all, how is the Fed supposed to know when the market is "disorderly," and how is it supposed to know what kind of intervention is needed? In the end, the symptom of disorder always comes down to deviation of asset prices from some idealized norm. If sellers of the seven-year bond find that they have to make significant price concessions in order to attract buyers, the Fed is supposed to notice and step in as buyer, while at the same time selling other securities for which buying interest is stronger, say the two-year bond. Such intervention requires the Fed to have in mind a more or less clear norm indicating what current asset prices should be, so that it can use deviation from that norm as an indication of which issues it ought to be buying and which issues it ought to be selling.

In 1937, the more or less obvious idealized norm was something economists call the expectations hypothesis of the term structure (EH). According to this theory, the return on a long-term bond should be just an average of expected short-term interest rates over the life of the bond. The logic is simple. Suppose you have money that you want to invest for the next two years. You can either buy a bond with two years to maturity or you can buy a short-term bill with only one year to maturity and then reinvest the proceeds in another one-year bill. Since investors can freely choose between these two strategies, they must be equally attractive in market equilibrium; both two-year bonds and one-year bills have to be held willingly by someone. One measure of the attractiveness of an investment strategy is simply its yield to maturity. Accordingly, the EH suggests that the expected yield to maturity for each of the two investment strategies should be the same.

Appealing as this theory is, it cannot be the whole story because in actual fact the term structure typically slopes upward. Short-term interest rates are typically lower than long-term interest rates, so a long-term investment typically yields more than a series of short-term investments. One way to understand this apparent anomaly is that investors are influenced by something other than expected yield to maturity. Maybe the long-term investment is more risky in some way, and the extra yield is compensation for bearing that risk? Certainly it is true that long-term investments can potentially fluctuate in value much more widely than short-term investments, but this fluctuation matters only if for some reason you have to sell before maturity. This line of thinking thus suggests that the extra yield on the long-term investment is a kind of "liquidity premium" that compensates the long-term investor for the fact that he may have to take a loss if for some reason he needs to convert his investment into cash before maturity.

This way of thinking about the term structure was more or less state of the art in 1937, and the Fed's 1937 commitment to maintain orderly conditions in the money market can therefore be understood as a commitment relative to this norm. In 1937, the Fed's commitment meant that it would take the "liquidity premium" as given by the market, and ensure shiftability at that premium. Over time, interest rates would change, depending on market conditions. Short rates might rise or fall by more than long rates, making the term structure flatter or steeper, but that was not supposed to be any concern of the Fed. "Orderly conditions in the money market" meant smoothing price changes, including changes in the liquidity premium, not preventing them.

Why did the Fed think that such smoothing was an appropriate policy goal? Here, perhaps by analogy to previous experience with seasonal smoothing, the Fed seems to have understood itself as intervening to produce the outcome that the market was trying, unsuccessfully, to achieve. Behind this approach was the idea that, in a well-functioning market, private dealers themselves would be doing the smoothing, using their own balance sheets to absorb temporary imbalances of supply and demand. But even in a well-functioning market it might occasionally happen that the bulk of some particular security issue was locked away somewhere out of the reach of the dealers, so that the market price of that security came to reflect a scarcity premium. In such a case, the Fed could help the market by disgorging its own holding. If this problem could arise in normal times, then a fortiori during a depression, when private dealers were weakened and private investors reluctant to disgorge their only safe securities, the market could use the Fed's help. The Fed's April 1937 announcement was intended to signal that such help would be forthcoming.

Had events not intervened, this reassuring signal might have been the first step toward reconstruction of private capital markets on a new, more solid, foundation, based now explicitly on shiftability rather than self-liquidation. As the capitalization of the dealers was restored, the time would eventually have come when dealers themselves would have taken over the task of smoothing, leaving the Fed free to concentrate instead on general credit policy. In this respect, it is telling that, at the very same moment when the Fed was sending its reassuring signal about the shiftability of all government securities, it was also doubling reserve requirements in an effort to forestall a possible unhealthy credit expansion on the basis of the burgeoning excess reserves that had built up in the banking system. [2] In 1937, the Fed was preparing for return to normalcy.

What kind of normalcy might have been built on these new foundations? As mentioned earlier, the Fed's commitment to ensure shiftability brought to the forefront the whole question of capital asset pricing. The EH was a good starting point, especially as augmented by the idea of liquidity preference that generated risk premiums in the yields of longer-maturity assets. But matters would never have remained at such a primitive level. Once you start down the road of intervening to correct deviations from appropriate pricing, you also start down the road of constantly improving your theory of appropriate pricing, if only to protect yourself from profit-seeking counterparties on the other side of your trades.

Just so, the evolving role of the Fed inevitably would have led to further investigation of the foundations of the concept of "liquidity premium" in order to understand where it comes from, why it takes on particular values for particular instruments, and why those values change over time. In Britain, John Maynard Keynes and John Hicks were already showing a possible road forward with their "normal backwardation" theory of why long-term rates tend to be higher than short-term rates (see chap. 4). [3] Events intervened, however, and these early contributions got put on the shelf. The hoped-for restoration of private capital markets, and the institutional evolution that would have followed from that restoration, were both diverted, first by renewed economic downturn in 1938, and then by World War II.

Monetary Policy and the Employment Act

During World War II, the Fed once again took on responsibility not only for maintaining orderly markets in government debt, but also for fixing prices of that debt. Private capital markets essentially disappeared and were replaced by an expanded market for government debt, for which the Fed served as market maker. As new credit went preferentially to government, businesses and households used any excess funds first to pay down their own debts, and then to accumulate government debt. After the war, at the insistence of the Treasury, the Fed continued to fix prices, with the result that government bonds served essentially as a kind of interest-bearing cash. So flush was the private sector with its accumulation of war debt that reconstruction of private capital markets could and did wait until these wartime accumulations had been drawn down.

Meanwhile, the Employment Act of 1946 crystallized the new political consensus in favor of using the power of the federal government "to promote maximum employment, production, and purchasing power." The experience of wartime spending had produced a new appreciation of the power of fiscal measures to pull the economy out of depression, while the experience of wartime wage and price controls had produced a new appreciation of the power of direct measures to stem even very powerful inflationary pressures. Even more, the experience of low and stable interest rates during the war had produced a new appreciation of the power of finance to support important social goals. In all these dimensions, wartime lessons shaped postwar understanding of economic policy in ways that involved a significant downgrade of the role of monetary policy and the Fed. The Employment Act made no mention of a possible role for the monetary authorities in achieving the new goals; in practice the role of the Fed was limited to fixing the price of government debt for a full five years after the Employment Act was passed.

Nevertheless, inside the Fed, preparations were being made for a return to normalcy. The first step was to regain control over short-term interest rates. Pegged at only 3/8 percent during the war, when long bonds were supported at the more generous rate of 2½ percent, the short-term bill had attracted very little private interest, with the consequence that the Fed wound up owning almost all of the outstanding bills. By raising short-term yields on assets it already owned, the Fed was finally able to attract private buyers and so to begin the process of rebuilding a proper money market. After a few years of this, in 1951 the Fed was also finally able to rid itself of responsibility for pegging bond prices. Under the new Fed chairman William McChesney Martin, this abdication of wartime responsibility was presented as a crucial step toward rebuilding a proper money market for use in postwar monetary policy intervention. The key document was the 1952 report of the FOMC's Ad Hoc Subcommittee on the Government Securities Market, a committee chaired by Martin. [4]

In retrospect, this report, and the "bills only" doctrine that emerged from it, can be understood as an adaptation of the FOMC's 1937 commitment (to maintain "orderly conditions in the money market") to the significantly changed conditions of 1952. In both cases, the central idea was to support rebuilding of the dealer infrastructure of private capital markets. In 1937, the Fed thought it could confine its involvement to the government securities market, and it relied on private dealers to bring orderly conditions to private capital markets as they recovered. By 1952, however, the government market was more or less the entire capital market and the private dealer system was essentially moribund. It seemed to follow that the task of rebuilding the infrastructure of private capital markets had to begin at a more primitive stage by first attracting private dealers to act as market makers in the government securities market.

"Bills only" was thus a way of signaling that the Fed was leaving the long end of the market to the private dealers. (It was of course also a way to avoid political pressure to keep long rates low and stable.) Thenceforth the Fed would maintain orderly conditions at the short end, and rely on arbitrage and the private dealers to bring orderly conditions to the long end. In 1937, the EH had served as the norm for the Fed's own intervention across the term structure of Treasury debt. In 1952, the same EH was to serve as the norm for private profit-maximizing dealers.

In practice, even this simple idealized norm proved to be unrealizable in the rigid financial conditions inherited from New Deal reforms. Regulatory constraints on portfolio investment created demand for specific issues that was not readily diverted into other issues by mere price movements. Thus, although deviations from the EH norm offered profit opportunity for dealers, exploiting those opportunities was possible only if the dealers were prepared to hold the resulting position to maturity; the very existence of such deviations was a sign that the position would not be easy to liquidate. Assets that theory treated as close substitutes, and thus ideal candidates for arbitrage, were in fact not close substitutes at all in the portfolios of the ultimate wealth holders, and hence not for anyone else either.

Allan Sproul, the president of the New York Fed, had anticipated exactly this problem and thus had spoken out in opposition to "bills only." [5] He thought the Fed should retain its ability to operate in each of the multiple fragmented and disconnected credit markets, as well as in the long end of the Treasury market. Experience of the new policy proved him right, but only in the short run. Over the longer run, the vision of institutional arrangements laid out by Martin in the 1952 report proved remarkably prescient, as we shall see. It just took longer than he anticipated.

Meanwhile, the next step for the Fed after regaining control over interest rates was to revive its own role in managing them. We have seen how, during the 1920s, following the Strong rule, the Fed targeted borrowed reserves as a measure of money market tightness and slack, and used open market operations to increase or decrease borrowing depending on whether it felt that conditions warranted a bit more discipline or a bit more elasticity. In the 1950s, the Fed adopted a quite similar procedure, based on a quite similar theory. The only difference was that now it targeted so-called free reserves, defined as the difference between excess reserves and borrowed reserves. [6]

This operational change can be understood, first of all, as a nod to the developing federal funds market, in which banks with excess reserves were increasingly able to lend their excess to banks with deficient reserves. Such interbank lending had the effect of decreasing both the sum of excess reserves and the sum of borrowed reserves by the same amount. One advantage of the free reserves concept, therefore, relative to the former focus on borrowed reserves alone, was that it was not affected by fluctuations in the volume of interbank lending in the federal funds market.

Another advantage was that the free reserves concept could be either positive (in times of slack) or negative (in times of tightness). By contrast, the borrowed reserve concept seemed to have a natural floor at zero since, once no bank was borrowing reserves from the Fed, there was no way for the Fed to "make discount rate effective." (During the early years of the Depression, this apparent floor had led the Fed erroneously to conclude that monetary conditions were maximally expansive.) The new procedure recognized that, even when no bank was borrowing from it, the Fed could still exert additional downward pressure on short-term interest rates by buying securities outright; the effects of such open market operations would show up as an expansion of free reserves.

As in the 1920s, the purpose of the Fed's post–Fed-Treasury Accord operations was not merely to ensure orderly conditions in the money market, but also to contribute to economic stabilization more generally by constraining speculative excess on the upside and by supporting markets during liquidation on the downside. In 1955, addressing a joint meeting of the American Finance Association and the American Economic Association, New York Fed president Sproul explicitly endorsed the goals of the Employment Act, and urged the importance of the Fed for achieving those goals: "We must be alert to oppose both inflationary and deflationary pressures, either one of which can upset the precarious balance of a high-employment, high-production, high-income economy." [7] In the same address, Sproul also asked the assembled academics for their help: "It seems to me that this matter of open market techniques involves problems of economic significance beyond its immediate technical application, and that it deserves your study and your published findings. [8]

Listening to the Academics

Be careful what you ask for. Academic advice had not always been welcomed by the Fed, and for good reason. During the 1920s, the Yale economist Irving Fisher had spearheaded a campaign to pass legislation that would have required the Fed, as a matter of law, to stabilize the price level. Fisher's analysis rested on his version of the quantity theory of money, developed in his 1911 book *The Purchasing Power of Money*. According to Fisher, both inflation and deflation could easily be avoided simply by manipulating the money supply. Since they could be avoided, they should be avoided, both as a matter of justice between creditors and debtors and as a matter of efficiency in economic behavior. When price levels shift around, he argued, people tend to make mistakes in their economic decisions because they fail to distinguish movements in individual prices (which signal changes in profit opportunities) from movements in the price level (which contain no such signal). These mistakes, which he called "money illusion," he thought were an important cause of business fluctuations. Thus, he concluded, a policy of manipulating the money supply in order to stabilize the price level should also help to stabilize the economy more generally.

In the 1920s, the Fed had resisted Fisher's attempt to tie its mission explicitly to price stabilization, but not because of any particular objection to price stabilization as a goal. Rather, it rejected the idea that such stabilization was as easily achieved as Fisher thought, and rejected furthermore the idea that manipulation of the money supply was the most efficient operational mechanism toward that end. The yawning gap between Irving Fisher of Yale and Benjamin Strong of the New York Fed was not so much about the mission of the Fed as it was about the gap between academic monetary theory and central banking practice. For Strong, the focus of attention was not so much on the quantity of money as it was on the price of credit, which is the rate of interest. Strong's idea was that the pace of lending depends on the profitability of lending, which is the difference between the loan rate of interest and the money market rate of interest. Central bank intervention thus properly focused on the money rate of interest, using control over bank reserves as leverage, to influence the pace of lending.

In the 1920s, emergent central banking practice (Strong) easily trumped a priori academic monetary theory (Fisher), but only to be itself trumped by depression and war in the 1930s and 1940s. The result was a substantial downgrading of monetary policy, in both academic and policy circles. In the 1950s, when peace and then prosperity returned, so too did the old debate, albeit in somewhat different form and with different protagonists.

In academia, Milton Friedman, professor of economics at the University of Chicago, reprised Irving Fisher with his proposal to require the Fed to stabilize, not prices directly, but rather the growth of the money supply. [9] Three percent, said Friedman, was about right to achieve long-run price stability, given historical patterns of long-run growth in the real economy. For our story the important point is that, in a nod to the weak empirical connection between money and prices in the short run, Friedman advocated abandoning the goal of active countercyclical stabilization. In this respect, Friedman's monetarism diverged from Irving Fisher's, and in a direction that took him even further away from central banking practice; the postwar gap between academic theory and central banking practice threatened to yawn even larger than the prewar gap.

Meanwhile, reprising Benjamin Strong at the Fed, Allan Sproul and William McChesney Martin quite definitely saw a role for countercyclical monetary policy ("leaning against the wind"). The difference from the 1920s was that, after the Employment Act, the commitment to economic stabilization was much more widely held, and a broader range of instruments was available for the task. Monetary policy no longer had to do everything, so central bankers could pick and choose those dimensions of the stabilization project for which their instruments were best suited. By stabilizing money markets, the Fed could do its own bit toward the broader social goals of stabilizing the price level and economic activity more generally. Friedman's monetarism was definitely not the kind of academic work that Sproul had meant to encourage.

Closer to what Sproul probably had in mind was the work of John G. Gurley and Edward S. Shaw, who reprised Harold Moulton in their 1960 book *Money in a Theory of Finance*. Moulton, it will be recalled, had sparked the reconceptualization of liquidity as shiftability, arguing that the shiftability concept was better suited to American conditions in which banks were much more involved with long-term capital finance. Taking their theme from Moulton, Gurley and Shaw expressed concern that bank regulations introduced during the New Deal were having the unintended consequence of suppressing capital accumulation. New financial intermediaries, especially pension funds and insurance companies, were taking over the role formerly played by banks, but inadequately so. The liquidity preference of households meant that they still tended to channel their savings preferentially to the relatively safe and liquid liabilities of banks.

In the Gurley-Shaw idealization, each financial intermediary issues a characteristic type of liability that attracts funds from a distinct segment of final savers, funds that the intermediary then uses to acquire a characteristic type of asset issued by a distinct segment of final borrowers. This image of the institutional organization of financial markets was intended to capture the rigidities that had been built into the American financial system by regulatory strictures (the very rigidities that Sproul had emphasized in his opposition to "bills only"), but Gurley and Shaw went further. Regulatory constraints on banking meant that asset holders were not able to find in the marketplace sufficient assets to satisfy their liquidity preference, and the consequence was higher liquidity premiums than necessary, which stifled general capital accumulation and long-run growth. Furthermore, attempts by the central bank to manage money by managing bank credit risked stifling those particular forms of capital accumulation that were most reliant on bank credit. In both respects, long-run growth was being sacrificed to short-run cyclical stabilization; the Fed could do better.

At the Fed and in academia, the decade of the 1950s was devoted largely to monetary reconstruction, in terms of both institutional structures and intellectual frameworks. In both respects, by 1960 we were more or less back to 1930; money mattered again. Given the enormous discredit that had befallen both the Fed and monetary economics during the 1930s, it was a tremendous achievement. But getting money back on the agenda was only the beginning, since meanwhile the world had moved on. The problem after 1960 was to find a way to integrate the new appreciation of money within the larger institutional and intellectual framework of macroeconomics, which had undergone tremendous change in the decades since 1930.

Monetary Walrasianism

One way to understand the catastrophe of the Great Depression is not so much as a failure of monetary policy narrowly but rather as a failure of the decentralized market system more generally. Price determination in response to the fluctuation of supply and demand was apparently not sufficient to ensure satisfactory performance of the economy as a whole. The experience of instability and unemployment was unacceptable, and the consequence was an opening to explore alternatives, both institutional and intellectual. One possible alternative was to abandon the market economy entirely and replace it with a centralized command economy; the success of the U.S. war economy showed well enough that such a possibility could work. But maybe there was another way, a middle ground in which government managed rather than commanded. The commitment to exploring that middle ground is what the so-called Keynesian revolution was all about, at least in the United States.

We have seen already how the Fed's 1937 commitment to maintain "orderly conditions in the money market" makes sense only by reference to an idealized norm, at that time the liquidity-augmented expectations hypothesis of the term structure. No less did the broader 1946 commitment "to promote maximum employment, production, and purchasing power" make sense only by reference to an idealized norm. By 1960, when money finally came back into the picture, economists and policymakers had already chosen the ideal norm against which to compare imperfect reality. That norm was the general equilibrium model first put forth by Léon Walras in 1874.

It seems to have been John Hicks, first in his 1937 article "Mr. Keynes and the 'Classics'" and then in his 1939 book *Value and Capital,* who most clearly set forth the general equilibrium model of Walras as the idealized norm against which to calibrate real world deviations. Walras famously envisioned the economy as a set of simultaneous equations, each one setting the supply of a particular commodity equal to the demand for that commodity. The equilibrium of the system is the set of prices that satisfies all of the equations simultaneously. By 1960, Arrow and Debreu had developed the Walrasian general equilibrium idea into a fully rigorous mathematical formalism, but their version of the model had a problem; there was no place in it for money. [10]

Those who wanted to bring money into the picture had therefore to find a different starting point, which they did in a 1938 article by Jacob Marschak titled "Money and the Theory of Assets." Here is the origin of monetary Walrasianism, the operational form taken by the Keynesian revolution in terms of money. The idea was, by analogy to Walras, to treat the financial side of the economy also as the solution to a set of simultaneous equations, each one involving the supply and demand for a particular financial asset, money being only one of many such assets. [11]

It took a while for the Marschak approach to gain acceptance, in part because of war, and because of monetary discredit too. But in 1952 Harry Markowitz reprised the Marschak approach in his seminal "Portfolio Selection," and in 1958 James Tobin used the approach to develop a theory of money demand in "Liquidity Preference as Behavior towards Risk." [12] Once these works demonstrated the apparent viability of the new approach, the next question was how to bring the new approach to money into contact with the institutional specificity of the American economy as emphasized by Gurley and Shaw, on the one hand, and with the practical stabilization policy goals as emphasized by Sproul and Martin, on the other hand. That's what James Tobin, among others, was doing during the decade of the 1960s, work summed up in his 1969 "A General Equilibrium Approach to Money."

In fact, Gurley and Shaw had already paved the way for Tobin's monetary Walrasianism by presenting household liquidity preference as a matter not just of money demand but also more generally of portfolio choice. In the Gurley and Shaw framework, the institutional specificity of the American economy involved various distortions in the supply of assets, while the price of assets moved to ensure that all assets were held by someone. For Tobin, these distortions were the source of deviations from the ideal, but they were also the source of leverage for policymakers attempting to get closer to the ideal. Just so, Tobin would emphasize how the ability of the monetary authority to affect asset prices and hence real activity stemmed from the fact that "the interest rate on money is exogenously fixed by law or convention." [13] Other institutional rigidities, such as "prohibition of interest on demand deposits and a ceiling on time deposit interest," provided additional sources of policy leverage.

In effect, Tobin used Gurley and Shaw to bridge the gap between academic theory and central bank practice, but once the bridge was built the traffic that flowed over it was largely from academic theory to practice, not the other way around. In Tobin's hands, the Gurley-Shaw vision merely enriched the specification of the standard Hicks-Hansen IS/LM model, used by everyone for short-run comparative statics exercises. [14] Tobin's paper concludes, "There is no reason to think that the impact [of monetary policies and other financial events] will be captured in any single exogenous or intermediate variable, whether it is a monetary stock or a market interest rate." This is a potshot both at academic monetarists who focus attention narrowly on the money stock and at central bank practitioners who focus attention narrowly on the money rate of interest. It is also an attempt to make common cause with the Sproul/Martin conception of the role of the Fed as stabilizer of the financial sector quite generally.

The Marschak-Tobin framework thus became the template for monetary practice as well as theory, once it got operationalized as the financial sector of the Fed's large-scale econometric model of the United States. [15] The idea was to build an empirically calibrated model of how all the various possible levers of government policy affect variables of economic interest—such as output, employment, and capital investment—with a view to informing the use of those levers. Monetary policy was to be conceived broadly as encompassing any and all levers involving the financial sector of the economy. It was the high point of the age of management, when the new Keynesian economic science seemed to show how it was possible, merely by manipulating a few strategic policy levers, to achieve the ambitious goals of the 1946 Employment Act.

In all the excitement, no one seems to have noticed that the monetary Walrasianism of Tobin amounts to nothing less than an apotheosis of the shiftability view of the nature of liquidity. Notwithstanding institutional rigidities on supply, all assets in Tobin's model are assumed to be salable at a price determined by the balance of supply and demand. In effect, market liquidity is assumed for all assets equally. The demand for money is not a demand for the ultimate *liquid* asset but only a demand for the ultimate *riskless* asset, as all assets are assumed to be liquid.

Recall that the Arrow-Debreu version of Walras could not be used as a norm for monetary policy because there was no place for money in it. By contrast, the Marschak-Tobin version of Walras had something in it that could be labeled money, but it had a different problem, namely, abstraction from liquidity as the defining feature of money. The Marschak-Tobin idealization posed no immediate problem in the rigid institutional setting of the immediate postwar period; after all, the overwhelming majority of financial assets were government securities, and all of them were fully and equally liquid because of the Fed's backstop. But once rigidities were relaxed and private capital markets restored, the abstraction from liquidity would become increasingly problematic.

Tobin himself hints at what was to come. In his 1969 model, all policy levers depend on institutional rigidities, so what happens if those rigidities are ever relaxed, as they would be over the coming decades? Tobin was presciently clear. "There would be no

room for discrepancies between market and natural rates of return on capital, between market valuation and reproduction cost.
There would be no room for monetary policy to affect aggregate
demand. The real economy would call the tune for the financial
sector, with no feedback in the other direction." [16] Thus, according to Tobin's *own model*, once rigidities are relaxed the ideal norm
would be realized without any policy intervention. Crucially, that
ideal norm was the full market-clearing Walrasian equilibrium, a
model with no place for money.

For the present story, the important point is that the ideal
norm that emerges when all rigidities are relaxed is a world in
which liquidity is a free good. In that ideal world everything, both
real commodities and financial assets, is perfectly shiftable. This
is the norm against which reality was to be measured and toward
which policy intervention was to be directed. As a measure of how
unreal and unreachable that norm was, it is sufficient to note that,
in this ideal world, the EH holds true, even without any liquidity-
premium add-factors. Nevertheless, that was the ideal and so it
became the Fed's job to achieve it. Since the ideal was a world in
which liquidity is a free good, it seemed to follow that the job of
the Fed was to supply liquidity as a free good.

A Dissenting View

In historical retrospect, we can appreciate that the Marschak-
Tobin framework was not the only possible road forward; the road
not taken was a reconstructed money view. Unlike the Marschak-
Tobin model, the logic underlying classic central banking practice
did not depend on any rigidities or inefficiencies. Instead, classic
central banking literature developed a theory of bank rate management that rested ultimately on the role of the central bank as

lender of last resort in times of crisis. Understanding the origin of crisis as a matter of the inherent instability of credit, classic central banking practice sought to intervene before the crisis to prevent buildup of speculative excess. True, American banking practice was different, and as a consequence American central banking practice came to focus more on open market operations than on discount operations. Nevertheless, the classic vision of the central bank's problem and mission could have been adapted simply by focusing on the Fed's ability to use its control over funding liquidity to influence market liquidity.

In the American academy, the most prominent voice that retained contact with the older traditions of central banking thought was that of Hyman Minsky, professor of economics at Washington University in St. Louis. [17] A student of Joseph Schumpeter at Harvard, Minsky placed at the center of his own thought Schumpeter's idea that the capital development of the nation was crucially dependent on the organization and operation of the financial system, and particularly the banking system. Minsky's first published paper, on "Central Banking and Money Market Changes" (1957) represents the earliest attempt by any academic to grapple with the implications of new money market instruments, specifically in the federal funds and repo markets, for the operational effectiveness of the Fed.

The elasticity provided by these markets would, Minsky suggested, ultimately undermine attempts to use monetary policy for aggregate stabilization, but would nevertheless leave in place the older and more fundamental central bank function as lender of last resort. Even as the American academic discussion was getting organized around a debate between monetarists (Milton Friedman) and Keynesians (James Tobin), Minsky was working to carve out a third position that reformulated classic British central banking practice for modern American conditions. Minsky's source for understanding British practice was not Hawtrey but rather Richard Sayers, whose magisterial history *Bank of England Operations, 1890–1914* explained how the vanished prewar system had worked. Nevertheless, Minsky's conclusion, which he termed the "Financial Instability Hypothesis," has more than a little flavor of Hawtrey insofar as the emphasis is on the inherent instability of credit.

The credit that concerned Minsky was not Hawtrey's merchant trade credit but rather business investment credit, bank lending to finance capital investment spending by American business. When businesses borrow, they commit themselves to a stream of future payments, and their ability to make those payments depends on realizing a net positive cash flow from their investment. The *solvency* of a business depends on the balance between the current valuation of payment commitments (liabilities) and expected cash flows (assets). The *liquidity* of a business, however, depends on the match between the time pattern of those payment commitments and realized cash flows. The basic problem in a capital-using economy is that illiquidity is a fact of life, given that long-lived capital assets are the source of so much realized cash flow. Such capital assets generate cash flow only over an extended period of time, which means that liquidity is always a problem for the economy as a whole, and hence for each agent within the economy as well.

For Minsky, the inherent instability of credit is all about the shifting balance between cash commitments and cash flows. "Hedge" finance structures, in which promised future cash commitments are always less than realized cash inflows, are inherently stable; a business financed in such a way can never run into liquidity problems and therefore can focus its attention on other matters. The problem is that, over time, hedge structures tend to be replaced by speculative and then Ponzi finance structures, in which firms promise payments that they cannot necessarily

meet from concurrent cash flow. In good times, these more fragile finance structures cause no trouble; when the promised debts
come due, they are just rolled over to a future date. But the fragility is there nonetheless, since any dislocation in the refinance
mechanism can cause disruption. When the dislocation comes,
the size of the resulting disruption depends on the prevalence of
speculative and Ponzi finance structures that are vulnerable to
such a dislocation.

Why the tendency toward fragility? The reason ultimately is
the liquidity preference of wealth holders. Unwilling to tie their
money up for the life of the real capital asset they are financing,
investors are willing to accept a lower promised yield in order to
acquire a shorter-dated financial asset. In this way, they essentially
bribe borrowers to accept some part of the liquidity risk inherent
in long-term capital investment (everything after the maturity of
the note), while they take the rest (everything before the maturity
of the note). For the lender, having made the loan, the only way
to get his money back faster is to sell that loan to someone else;
this is *market liquidity*. For the borrower, having committed to the
series of payments specified in the loan, the only way to put off
those payments when they come due is by paying someone else
to make them, that is, by rolling debts as they come due; this is
funding liquidity.

In Minsky's thought, the tendency toward fragility comes from
the interaction between asset valuation and creditworthiness.
Whereas Hawtrey emphasized the valuation of inventories and
the feedback of that valuation on the availability of trade credit,
Minsky emphasized the valuation of capital assets and the feedback of that valuation on the availability of capital credit. Credit-
financed spending by one person creates income for others, both
present and prospective income, and the capitalization of that income raises asset prices and thus improves creditworthiness for

another round of spending. The resulting instability is more substantial than anything Hawtrey ever imagined, simply because the price of capital assets has a lot more room to move than the price of inventories. That wide range of price movement makes it also more difficult to control instability with mere interest rate policy.

In such a world, the best thing to do, according to Minsky, was to use collateral policy at the central bank's discount window to discourage speculative financing structures and to encourage hedge financing structures. If people know that only hedge financing structures will be eligible for discount when a crisis comes, that will tend to mute somewhat the push toward fragility on the way up, and hence also the scale of the collapse on the way down. Just as the Fed's operations in government debt had come to support the use of Treasury bills as a secondary reserve, so too would Fed operations in private hedge finance debt structures create a liquid market for that debt. In a crisis, that debt would move onto the balance sheet of the Fed, and once normalcy returned it would move back out.

That's how the world looked to Minsky, but not to either the monetarists or the Keynesians, whose debate dominated the academic airwaves. Their debate was all about managing aggregate fluctuations around a determinate equilibrium, and not at all about stemming the inherent instability of credit. Minsky's pessimism about the possibility of active management put him outside the optimistic Keynesian camp, and his pessimism about the inherent stability of a private credit economy put him outside the optimistic monetarist camp. Minsky's views were continuous with the great tradition of central banking thought, but that continuity proved to be a disadvantage in a postwar era looking to put the past behind it and build anew.

And so, instead of a Minskian reworking of central banking verities for modern circumstances, we got active money management along monetary Walrasian lines. In times of rising prices the Fed tightened monetary policy, causing money market interest rates to rise, thus creating incentive for private liquidity provision. As a consequence we got financial innovations such as the certificate of deposit, bank commercial paper, and Eurodollar borrowing. Higher rates also meant that refinance of maturing speculative positions was achieved only by pledging even greater future cash payments, which meant that even successful refinance tended to increase fragility. Thus, the natural thrust toward fragility was amplified, not dampened, by the operations of the financial authority. In a typical cycle, eventually refinance would become impossible for the most overextended units and crisis would erupt, forcing central bank intervention to mop up the mess ex post.

FOUR

The Art of the Swap

The pattern that Minsky was already noticing in domestic money markets in 1957, namely, financial innovation as a response to active money management, was also showing up in international money markets. Indeed, it was in the international money markets that the financial innovation most crucial for breaking down Depression-era rigidities first appeared. I refer here to the "swap," specifically the currency swap, which first made its appearance as a way to get around postwar controls on international capital flows.

After World War II, U.S. government debt was the coin of the realm internationally as well as domestically. The Bretton Woods agreement of 1944 ratified facts on the ground, the key facts being that the United States held not only most of the world's gold reserves but also most of its productive capital. Postwar Europe would be importing goods of all kinds from the United States and paying for them with dollars, so de facto the world trading system would be on a dollar standard. Nostalgia for the gold standard manifested itself as a nominal peg of the dollar to gold at $35 per ounce, but it was dollars that everyone needed, not gold. And it was dollars that everyone got, some granted (the Marshall Plan for reconstruction aid), some borrowed, and others earned by persistent undervaluation of foreign currencies relative to the dollar.

From the start, the Bretton Woods system was built on a contradiction. It established a fixed exchange rate system internationally even as it endorsed uncoordinated macroeconomic management at the level of the individual nation-state. The solution to this contradiction was supposed to be capital controls. Some countries might have loose macroeconomic policy while others might have tight macroeconomic policy. In order that the loose ones not be constrained by loss of international reserves, individual countries were permitted to control international capital flows, in and out.

The birth of the swap came as a way for individual firms to get around these national controls. The first such swaps were arranged as parallel loans, and this parallel loan construction remains the most straightforward way to understand them, even though in later developments the loans became implicit rather than explicit.[1] Indeed, the parallel loan interpretation is the most straightforward way to understand interest rate swaps and credit default swaps as well, two later constructions that played a key role in extending the logic of arbitrage throughout the evolving postwar financial system. The swap idea was completely central, and it all started with the currency swap, so it is of some importance to understand how this swap worked.

Currency Swaps and the UIP Norm

The essence of banking is a swap of IOUs. When a bank makes a loan, it adds to its balance sheet both an asset (the loan) and a liability (a deposit in the name of the borrower). The first currency swaps were nothing more than a minor variation on this traditional banking idea. Suppose an American company A has dollars but needs pounds in order to finance expansion by its subsidiary in England, and a British company B has pounds but needs dollars in order to finance expansion by its subsidiary in the United States. Suppose further that capital controls prevent them from trading currencies and making the desired investment directly. They can accomplish essentially the same thing by using a parallel loan construction.

Here's how. The American company loans its dollars to the subsidiary of the British company in the United States, while the British company loans its pounds to the subsidiary of the American company in Britain. No money ever travels across national borders so the letter of the law is respected. But although there are no *net* flows, any reasonable person would agree that the deal involves quite substantial notional *gross* flows, which offset; in effect, Company A and Company B evade the constraints that bind everyone else. We can represent the swap of IOUs as a set of entries on the balance sheets of the involved parties as follows.

Currency Swap as Parallel Loan

American Domicile				British Domicile			
Company A		*Subsidiary B*		*Subsidiary A*		*Company B*	
Assets	Liabilities	Assets	Liabilities	Assets	Liabilities	Assets	Liabilities
$ loan			$ loan		£ loan	£ loan	

What about credit risk? If all goes well, the American company will get repaid with dollars from the British company's subsidiary, but what if the sub doesn't pay? In that case, the American company instructs its own British sub to stop payment on the other leg of the swap, and the swap terminates. In effect, each loan serves as collateral for the other, so potential credit losses are limited. Premature termination thus does not involve outright loss, but it does leave the American company with no way to repatriate pounds earned by its foreign sub. For that, it would need to find a new British counterparty willing to swap.

One way to mitigate this kind of premature-liquidation risk is to insert a bank as the counterparty to each leg of the swap. Here, however, the parallel loan construction poses a problem, since each counterparty position would expand the bank's balance sheet by the size of the entire loan, thus attracting reserve requirements and absorbing scarce capital. The way out is to structure the deal as a swap of *implicit* IOUs, not actual IOUs; in this way our parallel loan construction becomes a currency swap.

Imagine that our two companies each do their swap not with each other but rather with J. P. Morgan, which has branches in both the United States and Britain. Company A promises to pay pounds and receive dollars from J. P. Morgan; Company B promises to pay dollars and receive pounds; J. P. Morgan promises to both pay and receive both dollars and pounds. Because everyone in this deal is both paying and receiving, we can book the deal not as a set of gross exposures (loans) but only as a set of net exposures (swap). The parallel loan construction remains, but only behind the scenes as below, where we use brackets to denote implicit IOUs.

Company A		J. P. Morgan		Company B	
Assets	Liabilities	Assets	Liabilities	Assets	Liabilities
[$ loan	£ loan]	[£ loan	$ loan]		
		[$ loan	£ loan]	[£ loan	$ loan]

In this arrangement neither A nor B has any exposure to early termination of the swap by the other. Only J. P. Morgan has that exposure, but J. P. Morgan has access to sources of liquidity that are not available to the individual companies. If one leg of the swap terminates early, J. P. Morgan need not scurry around looking for an alternative counterparty; it can easily hedge by swapping IOUs with another bank. Concretely, suppose that B terminates. Then J. P. Morgan looks for a counterparty, Bank C, willing to pay dollars (issue a deposit account liability) and receive pounds (hold a deposit account asset). If these deposits are implicit IOUs rather than actual IOUs, then we have what is called a forward exchange contract in which J. P. Morgan and Bank C commit to a future exchange of pounds and dollars at an exchange rate that is fixed today.

Company A		J. P. Morgan		Bank C	
Assets	Liabilities	Assets	Liabilities	Assets	Liabilities
[$ loan	£ loan]	[£ loan	$ loan]		
		[$ deposit	£ deposit]	[£ deposit	$ deposit]

Once hedging of this kind becomes readily available, J. P. Morgan can go the next step. Instead of merely *brokering* the swap between Company A and Company B, and adding its own counterparty credit enhancement, J. P. Morgan can begin to act as a true *dealer* by posting bid and ask prices for currency swaps, relying on the interbank market in Eurodollar deposits to hedge any mismatch in the resulting swap book. In this way, what began as a way of evading capital controls becomes over time simply a way of pricing loans. Companies borrow in whatever currency is cheapest for them, and then contract with a swap dealer to swap into whatever currency they need.

But why does Bank C provide the hedge? This is clearly the key to the whole thing, and not just for currency swaps but also for the interest rate swaps and credit default swaps that came later. Dealers will make markets in these swaps *only* if they can depend on Bank C to hedge any unmatched exposure on one side or the other. Presumably, Bank C provides the hedge because it expects to profit, but where does the profit come from? Let us look in more detail at the way the hedge works as a way of building intuition.

At the moment that Bank C swaps IOUs with J. P. Morgan, it trades a pound deposit for a dollar deposit at the prevailing spot exchange rate, $S = £/\$$. Then, over the time until maturity, each of these deposits accrues interest at the prevailing rate, $(1+r)$ for the dollar deposit and $(1+r^*)$ for the pound deposit. At maturity, therefore, Bank C will have a dollar liability of $(1+r)$ and a pound asset of $S(1+r^*)$. Its profit will thus depend on the prevailing spot exchange rate at maturity S_{+1}: profit = $\{S(1+r^*)/S_{+1} - (1+r)\}$. Note that, if the spot exchange rate is exactly $S_{+1} = S(1+r^*)/(1+r)$, then Bank C's profit is exactly zero. Denoting this no-profit exchange rate as F (for "forward" exchange rate), we can write Bank C's profit as $(1+r)\{F/S_{+1} - 1\}$. If the forward exchange rate is greater than the realized spot exchange rate, Bank C makes a profit; if less, it makes a loss. If the expectation of profit is what induces Bank C to enter into the contract in the first place, then it must be that the forward exchange rate is greater than the expected spot rate.

The point of all this is to show how the international currency swap market comes naturally to be organized around a particular arbitrage relationship, an idealized norm that economists call u covered interest parity (UIP).[2] Like the EH, UIP says that expected returns from two different investment strategies should be the same. Suppose you have money that you want to invest for three months. You can invest it in a dollar asset and earn the dollar rate of interest. Or you can convert it into foreign currency, invest at the foreign rate of interest, and then exchange the proceeds back into dollars. Since investors can freely choose between the two, they must be equally attractive. UIP interprets "equally attractive" to mean that the expected yield on these two investment strategies should be the same; any differential between the interest rates paid on the two investments should be exactly equalized by a change in the exchange rate. UIP says that the forward exchange rate should be equal to the expected spot rate.

But, like the simple EH, the simple UIP tends not to hold in practice, and our example of Bank C suggests why not. If UIP held, there would be no incentive for Bank C to provide the hedge that J. P. Morgan needs in order to square up its swap book. In effect, the failure of UIP is the source of expected profit that compensates speculators for the risk involved in absorbing mismatch in the currency swap market. Speculators such as Bank C are betting on the failure of UIP, borrowing in one currency and lending in another currency, and earning an expected profit as the reward for taking on the risk that exchange rates might move against them, producing a large loss.[3] The degree and the direction of the failure of UIP depend on the degree and the direction of the mismatch in the currency swap market. Although UIP fails, it remains the organizing norm in the sense that it would hold in the special case when there is no mismatch.

One implication of the UIP norm is that the only way the United States can sustain significantly lower interest rates than the rest of the world is if the dollar is expected to appreciate against foreign currencies. If, for whatever reason, that expectation is not held then investors will not be willing to hold dollars; in fact, they will want to convert their dollars into foreign currency. This was exactly the problem that the United States faced in 1961. In the immediate postwar period, most other currencies had been deliberately undervalued against the dollar in an attempt to ease transition from wartime conditions. As a consequence, by 1961, the dollar was coming under pressure and the peg of the dollar to gold was beginning to bite. To defend the gold value of the dollar against UIP arbitrage, the United States had to raise short-term interest rates, but that was the last thing the new Kennedy administration wanted to do, committed as it was to a policy of low interest rates in order to stimulate capital investment.

The famous 1961 Operation Twist was an attempt to have it both ways. The idea was that the Fed would raise short-term interest rates in order to support the value of the dollar but at the same time intervene in the long-term Treasury market in order to prevent the rising short rate from passing through into the long rate. Obviously, this amounted to an abandonment of Martin's "bills only" policy, but even more it also represented the first step toward replacement of the EH norm with the new Marschak-Tobin monetary Walrasian norm. (Not coincidentally, Tobin headed the Council of Economic Advisors under Kennedy, and in that position presided over the implementation of Operation Twist.)

Monetary historians report that Operation Twist was largely ineffective, in part because at the same time that the Fed was selling short-term Treasuries and buying long-term Treasuries, the Treasury was doing the reverse, so the net effect on the market as a whole was fairly minimal.[4] The significance of the operation, for our story, is that it rests at the same time on grudging *acceptance* of UIP as the norm in international money markets, and on willful *violation* of EH as the norm in domestic capital markets. By seeking to flatten the term structure of domestic interest rates, the policy amounted to an attempt to set the value of the term premium at a lower level than the EH norm would suggest. Instead of adapting itself to the market norm, the government was attempting to establish its own idealized norm, the norm that would be crystallized in Tobin's 1969 article "A General Equilibrium Approach to Monetary Theory."

As it happened, however, the swap technology that was originally developed to overcome regulatory rigidities in the international sphere turned out to be easily adapted to overcome regulatory rigidities in the domestic sphere as well. And as these rigidities were overcome, the EH norm would reassert itself as the natural organizing principle for domestic money markets, much as the UIP norm had already asserted itself as the natural organizing principle for international currency markets. In retrospect, the historical task of the Marschak-Tobin norm was to create the arbitrage opportunities that provided profit incentive for rebuilding a robust private dealer function.

Brave New World

Fischer Black, a computer expert working at the management consulting firm Arthur D. Little, was perhaps the first to see the future, as early as 1970: "Thus a long term corporate bond could actually be sold to three separate persons. One would supply the money for the bond; one would bear the interest rate risk; and one would bear the risk of default. The last two would not have to put up any capital for the bonds, although they might have to post some sort of collateral."[5] Today the world that Black was only imagining has become our reality, and the instruments he was only imagining have become our interest rate swaps and credit default swaps. Interest rate swaps came first, beginning in the 1980s; credit swaps are more recent, beginning in the 1990s. From the standpoint of modern finance, carving off these risks and selling them separately was the key to getting their prices right, and thus improving the efficiency of the system as a whole. From the standpoint of the money view, carving off these risks and selling them separately was the key to undermining the Marschak-Tobin norm for monetary theory and policy.

How does this "carving off" process work? Use of the term *swap* gives a clue that what is involved is some kind of swap of IOUs, in which one counterparty commits to make one stream of future payments and another counterparty commits to make a different stream of future payments. Behind the scenes, there is an implicit parallel loan construction, and we understand the swap better when we keep in mind that underlying construction.[6] Consider the risk exposure of the holder of a corporate bond after engaging in two such swaps of IOUs, as follows.

Mr. Investor		Mr. Default		Mr. Interest	
Assets	Liabilities	Assets	Liabilities	Assets	Liabilities
corporate bond					
[Treasury bond	corporate bond]	[corporate bond	Treasury bond]		
[Treasury bill	Treasury bond]			[Treasury bond	Treasury bill]

In the second line, Mr. Investor and Mr. Default swap implicit IOUs; this is the essence of a credit default swap (CDS). Investor promises to make the same payments that the corporation makes on its bond, and Default promises to make the same payments that the U.S. Treasury makes on its bond of the same maturity. Because the corporate bond typically pays a higher interest rate than the Treasury bond, Investor typically winds up making net payments to Mr. Default. These payments can be considered a kind of bond insurance premium since, in the event of default, Investor simply delivers the defaulted corporate bond to Default, receiving in return a perfectly good Treasury bond, or its cash equivalent.

In the third line, Mr. Investor and Mr. Interest swap implicit IOUs; this is the essence of an interest rate swap (IRS). Investor promises to make the fixed interest rate payments that the Treasury makes on its bond, and Interest promises to make the floating interest rate payments that the Treasury makes on a sequence of Treasury bills over the same horizon. Again, because the bond typically pays higher interest than the bill, Investor typically winds up making net payments to Interest. And again these payments can be considered a kind of insurance premium since, in the event that interest rates rise, Mr. Interest is on the hook for the capital losses on the bond.

The important point is that, if all works as planned, these swaps leave Investor with the same risk exposure as if he were holding a short-term Treasury bill instead of a long-term corporate bond. In Fischer Black's terminology, Investor is the one supplying the money for the bond, but he is not bearing any interest rate risk or credit default risk. Instead, Interest is bearing the interest rate risk; he has committed to pay the short-term interest rate even in the event that the short rate rises above the fixed rate that he is receiving. And Default is bearing the default risk; he has committed to make a series of fixed rate payments even if the corporation stops making payments on the corporate bond.

In recognition of this transfer of risk, we can treat Investor as the buyer of "protection" and book the swaps as assets for him and as liabilities for his counterparties. This convention is somewhat arbitrary because both swaps begin life as zero net value instruments; at origination the two implicit IOUs have exactly equal value. Later on, changes in the relative value of the two IOUs underlying the swap will inevitably shift the value of the swap into the money, on one side or the other. But the shift could go either way, and at origination no one knows which way it will go. Nevertheless, we adopt the convention that the buyer of protection books the swap as an asset, so we can show our implicit swap of IOUs alternatively as follows.

Mr. Investor		Mr. Default		Mr. Interest	
Assets	Liabilities	Assets	Liabilities	Assets	Liabilities
corporate bond					
CDS			CDS		
IRS					IRS

The important point is that, because the swaps were arranged not as a swap of actual IOUs but rather as a swap of implicit IOUs, they were not treated as loans for regulatory purposes. As such, swaps provided a natural way to get around regulations designed for traditional bank balance sheets, regulations that typically scaled both required reserves and required capital to the size of the balance sheet. Here is the origin of the so-called shadow banking system. In this regard, note that Mr. Interest is in effect borrowing short-term and lending long-term, just like a bank, and is thus exposed to both liquidity and solvency risk just like a bank, but without the associated regulatory apparatus or support—no backup liquidity support from the Fed, and no backup solvency support from the FDIC. If the short-term interest rate rises above the contracted fixed rate, Mr. Interest will find himself having to come up with liquid funds to pay out on his (implicit) short-term liability, even as the value of his (implicit) long-term asset has fallen, leaving him with a capital loss as the swap moves into the money on the side of Investor.

It follows that Investor's risk hedge is only as good as his counterparty. This counterparty risk can be managed by requiring that Interest (and Default) post "margin" to ensure performance—this is the collateral that Fischer Black was talking about—but the counterparty exposure remains. If the value of the swap moves by more than Interest (or Default) can tolerate, exhausting their ability to post collateral, the continued viability of the risk transfer depends on the counterparties being able to cap their losses by engaging in an offsetting swap with someone else. In the brave new world of modern finance, risk management ultimately depends on liquid swap markets, and liquidity means shiftability.

Now, as the previous discussion of currency swaps has made clear, the source of market liquidity in the swap market is the swap dealer who makes a two-way market by quoting both bid and ask prices. In the absence of such a dealer, if a counterparty defaults before the end of the contract, whatever risk was being transferred by the contract reverts to its original holder, who must look around for another counterparty. Swap dealers take on this rollover risk by standing in between the ultimate counterparties. Just as in the case of currency swaps, the liquidity of the IRS and CDS markets depends on a dealer infrastructure that makes two-way markets in these swaps. And just as in the case of currency swaps, the willingness of dealers to make markets depends on their ability to hedge the mismatch in their swap book.

For the interest rate swap case, the Eurodollar forward market and the closely associated Eurodollar futures market provide a natural hedge.[7] Imbalance in the underlying demand and supply of interest rate swaps thus shows up as an imbalance in the market for Eurodollar forwards and futures that pushes forward interest rates away from expected future spot interest rates. It is this gap that creates the expected profit needed to attract speculators to take up the overhang. The EH says that the forward rate should be an unbiased forecast of the future spot rate, but empirically the forward rate is typically higher than the future spot rate. One possible reason for this "anomaly" is a systematic overhang in net hedging demand; in this regard, the failure of EH in the interest rate swap case is comparable to the failure of UIP in the currency swap case.

For the credit default swap case, by contrast, there is no natural hedge available for dealers, and as a result the market has remained closer to a broker market than a proper dealer market.[8] Some individual corporate names attract wide interest, for one reason or another, and so are available for use as cross-hedges against positions in other individual names. Various *index* swap contracts, essentially fixed bundles of multiple names, also attract wide interest and so are available for use as a cross-hedge. But there remains no natural hedge for the index swap contract itself. Put simply, although *all* central banks are routinely interested in fostering market liquidity for government debt, *no* central bank is interested in fostering market liquidity for private debt. That is one of the things that will change once central banks recognize their new role as dealer of last resort, but until then the system is muddling along without a market liquidity backstop for private debt.

As a consequence, there is less ability for dealers to hedge net exposure in the credit default swap market, and there is correspondingly greater need to attract direct counterparties (i.e., speculators) by pushing the price of credit protection away from the level warranted by expected default. If more people want to buy protection than want to sell it, the price of protection must rise in order to attract speculative sellers, and vice versa if the imbalance is on the other side. The same logic that explains the failure of UIP and EH also explains the failure of the natural norm in the CDS market, namely, the tendency of the market price of a CDS to reflect expected future default probability. Indeed the mechanics of the CDS market reveal that there is even *more* reason to expect liquidity risk distortion in CDS pricing because of the lack of a natural hedge.

This price distortion would prove to be a crucial mechanism of the credit crisis, once the CDS technology got extended from corporate bonds to mortgage-backed securities (see chap. 6), but at its inception no one could see that far ahead. Rather, attention focused on the way that the development of swap markets (currency, then interest, and then default) operated to improve the efficiency of pricing, thus making credit more freely and cheaply available. The important point seemed to be that the prices of these different risk exposures were established in market exchange, not by bilateral negotiations between banks and their clients. A corporate bond came to be understood as nothing more than a bundle of risk exposures, each with its own price, and from there it was just a small additional step to use the observed market price of the various pure risk exposures to price the bond itself. The logic of arbitrage required it. Thus, over time, the logic of arbitrage came to rule everywhere, first currency, then interest, and then finally default.

From Modern Finance to Modern Macroeconomics

As the various arbitrage pricing norms began asserting themselves in the realm of practical pricing, they also began to assert themselves in the realm of theoretical understanding. The first step was the rise of modern financial theory, which sought to explain how the logic of arbitrage determines prices in financial markets. The second step involved a spillover of that new understanding from modern finance into modern macroeconomics.

Modern finance and Tobin's monetary economics share a common ancestry, from the prewar work of Jacob Marschak in his 1938 "Money and the Theory of Assets" to the postwar work of Harry Markowitz in his 1952 "Portfolio Selection." Thereafter, however, their paths diverged. Tobin used the Markowitz approach to develop a theory of money demand in his 1958 "Liquidity Preference as Behavior toward Risk," which he later extended into his 1969 "General Equilibrium Approach to Money." Meanwhile Bill Sharpe, a student of Markowitz, asked what asset prices would be in an economy where everyone behaved according to the dictates of Markowitz's model of portfolio choice. The result was the capital asset pricing model (CAPM), which ushered in modern finance.[9]

The key idea of the CAPM is that all capital assets are, in a certain formal sense, close substitutes for one another. Each one has its own expected return and its own individual risk, as measured by the variance of its return. But CAPM says that the price of the asset is affected not at all by its individual risk but only by its contribution to aggregate market risk, which is measured by the covariance of the asset's return with the market as a whole. According to CAPM, some stocks are more risky than others, but the covariance measure of risk puts all on the same footing, and the price of covariance risk is the same for all.

This CAPM idea was applied first to equity markets, but similar reasoning soon revolutionized thinking about fixed income and currency markets as well, with important consequences for older thinking such as the expectations hypothesis of the term structure and the uncovered interest parity theory of exchange rates. Those consequences all revolved around a shift in the understanding of risk. In the new CAPM formalization, it became impossible to conceptualize liquidity risk as a separate category of risk. The world of the new modern finance theory was a world in which both EH and UIP were expected to hold, even without any liquidity risk add-factor.[10]

In practice EH and UIP continued not to fit the data very well. But now empirical failure could be attributed to problems with reality, not problems with theory—to continuing inefficiency in market operation, not to counterfactual theoretical abstraction from liquidity risk. Even more, any deviation of market price from ideal theory could be read as an indication of arbitrage profit opportunity, the exploitation of which would make the market ever more perfect, which is to say, ever more in line with the norm of modern finance theory. Wherever there was an "anomaly" there was a carry trade to exploit it: borrow in low-interest-rate currencies and lend in high-interest-rate currencies, borrow in short-term markets and lend in long-term markets, borrow at the risk-free rate and invest in risky bonds. In all these trades, leverage came to be seen not as a multiplier of risk but merely as the way to harvest arbitrage profits, a way to buy low and sell high.

Significantly, all of these arbitrage trades depended on the availability of funding liquidity, which fluctuated over time. Easy money meant increasing leverage and shrinking carry margins; tight money meant decreasing leverage and widening carry margins. Theory said that none of these carry trades should be profitable in equilibrium, but in practice they were all profitable in the upswing and then unprofitable in the downswing, and all profitable as well on average over the cycle. Credit-fueled arbitrage was the form that Hawtrey's inherent instability of credit took in the brave new world of modern finance. But modern economists no longer read Hawtrey's books, or even Minsky's attempt to update the Hawtreyan money view for the world of postwar America. Both seemed equally out of date, swept away by the advances of modern financial theory.

A further casualty of the finance tsunami was macroeconomics, specifically the Marschak-Tobin framework for monetary theory. Tobin had developed the framework, it will be recalled, to aid government in its ambition to manage aggregate economic fluctuation. The idea was to conceptualize the problem of selecting appropriate policy levers, and the appropriate setting for each lever, as an empirical question amenable to scientific study. From the beginning, it was recognized that the answer to that empirical question would depend on the institutional structure of the economy. An underlying premise of the exercise, therefore, was that institutional change was slow enough to be discounted for policy purposes. This premise would provide the opening through which the new finance thinking entered macroeconomics.

There had always been voices warning that even though institutional change is slow, it should not be neglected, because the direction of institutional change will inevitably be influenced by whatever policy is chosen. Goodhart's Law, named after Charles Goodhart, longtime chief economist at the Bank of England, warned that any apparently stable statistical relationship will inevitably break down once you begin to rely on it for policy purposes.[11] Large-scale econometric models built on the Tobin framework were never anything more than a catalog of such purportedly stable statistical relationships.

The weakest entry in the catalog was the so-called Phillips curve, which showed an apparently stable statistical relationship between inflation and unemployment. Academic reputations were made and lost in the argument about whether that relationship could be relied on for policy purposes; could we "trade off" a bit more inflation for a bit less unemployment?[12] But the point of Goodhart's Law was more general, and indeed ultimately threatened the very foundations of the econometric project, as Robert Lucas, professor of economics at the University of Chicago, would point out in his famous critique of econometrics.[13] It is simply a logical mistake, argued Lucas, to treat the behavioral equations in an economic model as invariant to policy intervention, since agents should optimally use whatever they know about current policy practice when they are deciding how to behave. Change the policy rule and you change the behavior rule as well.

Both Goodhart and Lucas were, in effect, warning about the limits of economic management, but toward different ends. Goodhart's aim was to suggest that traditional central bank policy, meaning modest interest rate management in the tradition of Bagehot and Hawtrey, might ultimately prove to be more reliable than Milton Friedman's monetarist recommendation to stabilize prices by stabilizing the money supply. The Lucas critique, by contrast, seemed to apply to Goodhart's favored central bank policy as well.[14] Lucas's implication was that the entire countercyclical management project might be misconceived. Here is the origin of the new macroeconomics that sought to understand economic fluctuation not as a deviation from ideal Walrasian equilibrium but rather as the equilibrium response to an external shock.

Ironically, the basic point of the Lucas critique had actually been mooted by Tobin himself. If you take away all the rigidities in Tobin's model, then you are left with the market-clearing model of Walrasian equilibrium, in which model there is no role for countercyclical policy to improve welfare. To Tobin, as to most Keynesians, such a market-clearing model was not relevant for policy, on empirical grounds, and he has a point. Labor markets and goods markets alike seem to involve a lot more than the fluctuation of prices bringing momentary demand and supply into line with one another. But as a description of the *financial* side of economic reality, the assumption of substantial institutional rigidity seemed increasingly out of step with developments on the ground; increasingly, the market-clearing model seemed to be the relevant one.

The reason was arbitrage. If Regulation Q, for example, put a ceiling on the rate of interest that savings and loan institutions could pay on their deposit liabilities, the consequence was an incentive to create a new financial instrument, with the look and feel of a deposit account but with a different legal status, to which Regulation Q would not apply. Here is the origin of the money market mutual fund. Subsequently, whenever interest rates rose above the ceiling, funds would move from the regulated to the unregulated account, and borrowers and lenders would find one another outside the regulated sector, especially the largest and most sophisticated borrowers and lenders. Experience with this kind of "disintermediation," as it was called, produced political pressure from the regulated sector for equal treatment, pressure that was amplified by the voice of borrowers who did not have access to the unregulated sector and so were cut off when funds flowed elsewhere. The result was gradual relaxation of Regulation Q, and a similar dynamic led to relaxation of other New Deal–era regulatory strictures, as the acceptance of one financial innovation emboldened the invention of others.

The economic managers (such as Paul Volcker) worked hard to slow this dynamic, convinced as they were that regulatory rigidities were the central guarantors of safety and soundness, as well as the basis for policy leverage. But they could not stop it, mainly because of the key role of the dollar in the world financial system. As always, the logic of arbitrage dominated in the international markets, where borrowers and lenders met outside the reach of domestic regulators, and the large money center banks all established offshore offices in order to participate. These offshore offices then served as the entry point for the logic of arbitrage to flow back into the domestic system and whittle away at domestic regulation. It took a while, but even before deregulation proceeded to its ultimate conclusion, the effect was to create a parallel unregulated banking system alongside the traditional regulated system. In the parallel system, reality already matched the market-clearing model.

Such institutional change might have been expected to revive the Bagehot-Hawtrey tradition in monetary economics, since nothing in that tradition depends on rigidities. In retrospect, the interventions of Charles Goodhart at the Bank of England and of Hyman Minsky in the United States can be understood as attempts to do exactly that. At least in the United States, however, the triumph of the shiftability concept had left the old traditions behind. Notwithstanding the assumed institutional rigidities, all assets in Tobin's 1969 model are salable at a price determined by the balance of supply and demand; all are assumed to be shiftable. As a consequence, the elimination of institutional rigidities created room, not for the old wisdom to return, but rather for a new illusion to flourish, the illusion that liquidity is a free good in a world of perfect markets.

As in financial theory, so too in macroeconomic theory, the guiding norm was an ideal world with perfect liquidity. As in financial practice driven by the profit motive, so too in economic policy practice driven by a welfare motive, deviations between the ideal world and the real world were conceived as opportunities for arbitrage. Most important, monetary policy came to be seen as a matter of making liquidity in the real world the free good that it was in ideal theory. The result was a systematic bias toward ease by the monetary authorities, systematic bias that private speculators were only too happy to exploit for private profit. In effect, the monetary authorities became partners with the private speculators in a quixotic drive to make EH as true in reality as it was in theory.

FIVE

What Do Dealers Do?

You don't know what you've got till it's gone.

Liquidity is like that. One day you've got a nice portfolio of high-yielding fixed income securities, which you can easily finance by using the securities themselves as collateral to borrow in a deep and liquid wholesale money market. The next day, you can no longer borrow at any reasonable rate, and you can't sell your nice portfolio either at any reasonable price. Liquidity is gone, and it is about to take you away with it.

When this happens, there is a natural human impulse to blame your counterparties. After all, it was only because they were willing to lend to you that you were able to put together the portfolio that is now hemorrhaging, and the hemorrhaging would stop if only they started to lend again. Only yesterday, you had your pick of lenders and could play one off against the other in order to get the best deal, low rates and low haircuts both. Now all the lenders seem to be in cahoots against you, all of them withdrawing credit simultaneously even when they know, better than anyone else, what the consequences will be for you and your portfolio.

The impulse to personalize an existential threat is all too human, especially so when the threat comes from a direction where scientific explanation has yet to penetrate. Did my crops fail? My enemy has cast a spell. His crops too? The gods are punishing both of us. In this regard, the decision of both the economics and finance disciplines to abstract from the monetary plumbing behind the walls, the better to advance scientific understanding on other dimensions, has had fateful consequences for our ability to sustain rational discourse in the face of a systemic plumbing failure. If we don't educate ourselves about how the system works when it is working, we will have no framework for understanding what is wrong when it fails.

Fortunately, the money view perspective that we need is not completely gone, however suppressed it may be in academic and policy circles. In the private sector, traders and speculators have never lost sight of the crucial importance of the survival constraint; the market won't let them lose sight, and it reliably punishes those who ignore its warnings. Similarly, in the public sector, practical central bankers, who deal every day in the same world that traders and speculators inhabit, have never lost sight of their own ability to relax the survival constraint, and of their responsibility to deploy that ability wisely. Those who inhabit the world of academic economics and finance have the luxury to abstract from the plumbing behind the walls, but the plumbers who spend their days doing business inside the money markets, behind the walls, do not. It is the plumbers' worldview we must tap if we are to learn the lessons of the current crisis and to build a more robust system going forward.

Inside the Money Market

The logical origins of the money market can be traced, perhaps surprisingly, to the operations of a decentralized payments system. Consider an idealized world in which everyone has a deposit account and a line of credit at a single big bank. In this world, all payments would involve nothing more than entries on the books of the bank. Net depositor A pays net depositor B simply by ordering the bank to debit his account and to credit B's account, leaving total bank liabilities and assets unchanged. Note how even this simple transfer mechanism involves partial relaxation of the "survival constraint" that would otherwise constrain both A and B; A temporarily enjoys greater cash outflow than cash inflow simply by drawing down his deposits, while on the other side of the transaction B temporarily enjoys greater cash inflow than cash outflow, and uses the difference to accumulate deposit balances for the future.

Lines of credit at the single big bank allow further relaxation of the survival constraint. Now net debtor C can pay net debtor D by drawing on his credit line at the bank, increasing his own debt while reducing D's debt, leaving total bank assets and liabilities unchanged. But also net depositor A can pay net debtor D, causing total bank assets and liabilities to shrink; and net debtor C can pay net depositor B, causing total bank assets and liabilities to expand. These simple examples show how relaxation of the daily survival constraint depends on credit; some people can enjoy cash outflows greater than cash inflows *only because* other people are willing to enjoy cash inflows greater than cash outflows, and vice versa. It all works so long as cash inflows and outflows on the books of the single big bank are equal.

In the real world we do not have a single big bank, but rather a single integrated banking *system*, and the key to that integration is the money market. In our system, when net depositor A pays net depositor B, there is a debit to A's account at A's bank and a credit to B's account at B's bank, and there is a corresponding debit to the reserve account of A's bank and a corresponding credit to the reserve account of B's bank. Payments elasticity in our decentralized payments system thus depends on interbank credit to relax the "reserve constraint" facing individual banks; some can enjoy reserve outflows greater than reserve inflows (A's bank) because others are willing to enjoy reserve inflows greater than reserve out-flows (B's bank), and vice versa.

In our world, banks hold almost no reserves on account at the Fed—at least that was the case precrisis—and instead settle ac-counts largely by borrowing and lending in the money market. The central mechanism for this kind of interbank credit is the fed-eral funds (FF) market, in which banks borrow and lend deposits at the Federal Reserve in order to keep their net reserve balances near zero. Just so, in the transaction between A and B, total retail bank deposits do not change, but total interbank credit does be-cause A's bank borrows the reserves it needs from B's bank. Inter-bank borrowing and lending in the money market is the mecha-nism that makes it possible for our decentralized banking system to approximate the efficiency of a single big bank.

Person A		A's Bank		B's Bank		Person B	
Assets	Liabilities	Assets	Liabilities	Assets	Liabilities	Assets	Liabilities
−deposit			−deposit		+deposit	+deposit	
			+FF loan	+FF loan			

We could extend this analysis to cover the cases where C pays D, A pays D, and C pays B, and to consider also how the amount of interbank borrowing depends on the balance sheets of the banks that are involved. Sometimes we will get expanding inter-bank credit and sometimes contracting interbank credit; it all de-pends on the pattern of payments. But you get the point. It all works so long as cash inflows equal outflows in the banking sys-tem as a whole.

We could also extend this analysis to cover cases where the rel-evant banks are not members of the Federal Reserve System and therefore do not have access to the federal funds market. In that case, the necessary interbank borrowing might take place in the offshore Eurodollar market at the interest rate known as LIBOR (London interbank offer rate). In a further extension, we could cover cases where the payment does not involve the banking system at all, and hence involves no interbank lending at all, instead involving secured borrowing and lending in the repo market by A and B directly. In effect, A raises funds to make its payment by selling (temporarily) some asset, and B receives the payment by buying (temporarily) some asset, one borrowing and the other lending through the intermediation of some security dealer counterparty; once again, this involves expansion of money market credit.

These three money market instruments—federal funds, Eurodollars, and repo—are all close substitutes in the sense that they can be used to do much the same thing, but not everyone has equal access to them, so their interest rates can and do vary. Typically, the repo rate is less than the federal funds rate, and the federal funds rate is less than the Eurodollar rate, but the spreads are very small, just a few basis points. Textbooks have therefore studiously ignored them, building their analyses around the useful fiction that there is a single money market rate of interest, controlled unproblematically by the Fed as a policy variable.[1] During the crisis, however, these spreads widened to 100 basis points or more, offering prima facie evidence that the crisis was, at least in part, about unprecedented stress on the payments infrastructure. If you don't have acceptable collateral for repo borrowing and you don't have access to the federal funds market, then you have no choice but to bid up the LIBOR rate until someone is willing to lend to you. That is what happened repeatedly as the crisis unfolded.

Even in normal times, stress arises whenever the pattern of payments deviates from the usual so that unfamiliar counterparties have to find a way to come together as borrowers and lenders.

Since the payments system clears every day, there is always the possibility that the moment of clearing comes before the decentralized money market has found a way to equalize cash inflows and outflows. In that case, the balance sheet of the Fed is available through the discount window as the ultimate backstop. Using the discount window, the Fed stands ready to equalize cash inflows and outflows by lending (cash outflows) and borrowing (cash inflows) as needed. If for some reason A's bank and B's bank cannot find each other in the interbank market, they can meet through the intermediation of the Fed, with A borrowing and B lending.

A's Bank		Fed		B's Bank	
Assets	Liabilities	Assets	Liabilities	Assets	Liabilities
	+discount loan	+discount loan	+reserves	+reserves	

In modern arrangements, this public discount mechanism is intended to be a backstop only for individual necessity and only until a private interbank loan can be arranged; to provide incentive for rapid unwind the discount rate is set at a penalty 100 basis points over the federal funds target. Normally, therefore, the discount window is hardly used at all, since federal funds are cheaper. More commonly, whenever an unusual pattern of payments requires a *general* expansion of interbank credit, the Fed facilitates the expansion by adding reserves to the market as needed. The mechanism for these "open market" operations is repo lending to security dealers at the market repo rate, not a penalty rate like the discount window.

The Fed's goal is to act as much as possible before the stress actually occurs, so it intervenes daily in anticipation of pressure in the interbank market that might otherwise drive the federal funds rate away from the target. The effect of the Fed's open market repo

lending is to increase reserves at the dealer's bank for the term of
the repo loan, thus providing funds for that bank to lend (in the
interbank market) wherever they are needed to facilitate the pattern of payments. Daily intervention of this kind by the Fed can
thus be understood as the final piece of the money market mechanism that makes our decentralized banking system operate as if it
were a single big bank.

Fed		B's Bank		Security Dealer	
Assets	Liabilities	Assets	Liabilities	Assets	Liabilities
+repo	+reserves	+reserves	+deposits	+deposits	+repo

Funding Liquidity and Market Liquidity

Historically, as we have seen (chap. 3), the repo market predates
the federal funds market. Before the establishment of the Fed,
banks used a kind of primitive repo system to transfer funds
around the system in their own attempt to create a single-big-
bank approximation. The first line of defense for a bank running
short of cash reserves was interbank lending (so-called banker's
balances) analogous to today's Eurodollar lending. But after that,
private bonds of various kinds served as collateral for interbank
lending.[2] Here we find the historical origin of the connection between funding liquidity and market liquidity that is so central
to modern arrangements. To understand how that connection
works, we shift our focus away from banks' use of the money market to facilitate elastic payments, and toward security dealers' use
of the money market to fund provision of market liquidity.

 If there were no repo market, a security dealer that sought to
profit by quoting a two-way market in some security would have

to finance its inventory of securities with its own capital or a line of bank credit. With the development of the repo market, repo credit becomes the primary source of funding for dealers, with bank credit serving only as a private lender of last resort. (Bank loans to dealers are typically arranged at a spread over the effective federal funds rate, that spread being the bank's profit over its marginal cost of funds.) Market liquidity (shiftability) depends on the willingness and ability of dealers to make a two-way market, and that depends on the willingness and ability of dealers to borrow and lend in the wholesale money market.[3] In modern arrangements, the Fed serves as backstop to this dealer system both directly, through its daily funding operations in the repo market, and indirectly, through lender of last resort support for the banking system.

The following stylized balance sheets make clear how it all works. To bring in the role of arbitrage, I depict the security dealer as harvesting the liquidity premium in the term structure by holding a long position in the Treasury bond (shown as an asset) and a short position in the Treasury bill (shown as a liability). The dealer achieves these positions by quoting prices for both bonds and bills, both buying and selling prices, with an eye toward achieving a target portfolio that balances expected profitability against risk. (Given price quotes imply a specific target portfolio through their effect on order flow by the ultimate buyers and sellers of securities.) The dealer finances both positions with repo, using the bond as collateral for repo borrowing and accepting the bill as collateral for repo lending. Some of the dealer's repo borrowing is repo lending by the Fed, but most of it is repo lending by other agents not shown (such as corporations or money market mutual funds). The marginal source of dealer finance is lending by the banking system.

Fed		B's Bank		Security Dealer	
Assets	Liabilities	Assets	Liabilities	Assets	Liabilities
Treasury bills	reserves	reserves	deposits	Treasury bond	Treasury bill
repo lending				repo lending	repo borrowing
		loans			loans

Because we are concerned with issues of liquidity, not solvency, I abstract in these balance sheets from the net worth (or capital) of each of these three entities. For our purposes such capital is important not so much as a buffer against potential loss but rather as a constraint on the ability and willingness of dealers to provide market liquidity by expanding their balance sheets.[4] A profit-maximizing dealer will have in mind the expected profit from its term structure arbitrage and will weigh that profit against potential risk. One risk is that bond prices fall, which threatens capital loss and possible insolvency, but typically the dealer's more immediate concern will be not with solvency but with liquidity, because the quantity of overnight repo borrowing depends on the market value of bond collateral. Falling collateral values mean less available repo credit, and hence greater reliance on more expensive bank borrowing and/or the need to liquidate some portion of the bond inventory in a falling market. This liquidity risk, as we may call it, is what limits the dealer's ability and willingness to leverage a given capital base, and this limitation has important consequences for asset prices.

To see the consequences clearly suppose, hypothetically and counterfactually, that there were no such limitation. Then, so long as the expected profit on the term structure was positive, dealers would have an incentive to increase leverage, buying bonds and selling bills.[5] Competition among dealers would drive expected profit on the term structure arbitrage to zero, and the expectations hypothesis of the term structure would come into its own. This hypothetical and counterfactual world is, of course, the idealized world imagined by both economics and finance theory as a way of abstracting from features of the monetary system that do not interest them; it is a world in which there is no survival constraint, hence no liquidity risk, hence no liquidity premium in asset prices. It is a world without dealers.

In the real world there are dealers, and dealers face a very real survival constraint, but one consequence of the Fed's backstop of funding liquidity is to weaken the force of that constraint. The question is, by how much? Knowing that the Fed will intervene to stabilize the federal funds rate, dealers rationally shift their risk-return calculus in favor of taking larger positions in the term structure arbitrage, and such a shift can be expected to move the structure of asset prices closer to the EH theoretical ideal, *but not all the way*. There has to be some expected profit on the term structure arbitrage or no dealer would do it. In other words, the only way the EH theoretical ideal could ever be fully achieved would be to have the Fed itself do the necessary arbitrage, because only the Fed is limited by neither profit considerations nor a survival constraint. That may well be how things work in wartime (as we have seen) but it is not how things work in peacetime.

In peacetime, notwithstanding the Fed's backstop, the survival constraint limits dealer leverage and so maintains positive expected profit for the term structure arbitrage, on average, as well as for other forms of liquidity risk bearing. At any moment, the dealer has in mind a target portfolio that balances expected profit against liquidity risk, and quotes two-way prices in an attempt to achieve that portfolio. Anything that changes the target portfolio will therefore cause dealers to change the prices they quote.

In this regard, consider again the effect of expansionary open market operations, now from the perspective of the dealers rather than their clearing banks. Expansionary open market operations mean increased repo lending by the Fed to the dealers. The immediate effect is to increase the liquid funds available to the dealer, funds that substitute for expensive bank borrowing and thus facilitate an increase in the scale of the dealer's target portfolio—specifically, more long bonds. To achieve this new target portfolio requires increasing the price quoted for bonds. In this way, open market operations in the money market affect asset prices in the capital market immediately, through the risk-return calculus of the primary dealers.

This direct and immediate effect on asset prices can be contrasted with the indirect and lagged effect on the larger economy that economists usually emphasize, an effect that is supposed to operate through the incentive of banks to expand customer lending when they find themselves holding excess reserves. There can be no question which effect is the more immediate. Monetary policy works, in the first instance, by affecting the behavior of dealers, not banks, and by pushing around asset prices, not bank lending. Maybe eventually the lending mechanism kicks in, but on a timescale much longer than the daily survival constraint that is at the center of a money view perspective.

This account of how the system works is simplified and stylized, but we could easily extend it to include, for example, dealers who make markets in non-Treasury securities, and who therefore find themselves involved in other kinds of risk arbitrage. And we could also extend it to include dealers who do not engage directly with the Fed, since any general ease in funding conditions will affect their behavior as well. The general point is that, as the primary dealers change the prices they quote on Treasury bonds and bills in an attempt to influence their own order flow, other entities come to feel the effect of the Fed's intervention and they too respond by changing the prices they quote on other securities. Intervention in the money market thus affects not only (and maybe not even mainly) the Treasury bond price but also the price of corporate bonds, mortgage-backed securities, and even foreign securities.

We could also extend our analysis in another direction, to include other forms of intervention that might influence the dealer's risk-return calculus, and hence also asset prices. For example, because banks are lenders of last resort to the dealers, anything that affects the willingness and ability of banks to serve in that capacity will influence the dealers' estimate of risk and hence their willingness to expand the size of their positions on a given capital base. Indeed, the prospect of future liquidity availability may be more significant to a rational risk calculus than the availability of present liquidity that might well be temporary. Survival requires satisfying not only the present survival constraint but also all future survival constraints; any single failure can mean the end. In this respect, a public commitment to keep the federal funds rate low for an extended period operates as an encouragement for dealers to expand their balance sheets, an encouragement that can be expected to show up in asset prices today.

Anatomy of a Crisis

Suppose that there is a sudden shift, for whatever reason, in preferences by ultimate wealth holders in favor of money and against securities. Further suppose that the shift is not too large and not too long-lasting, so it can be readily absorbed by the dealer sytem as follows. Dealers buy the securities, financing their expanded balance sheets by borrowing from banks; banks expand dealer loans, financing those loans by expanding their deposit liabilities; and ultimate wealth holders satisfy their preference shift by holding the expanded deposit holdings. Call this a "normal crisis," a scaled-down version of a true crisis.

Wealth Holders		Dealers		Banking System	
Assets	Liabilities	Assets	Liabilities	Assets	Liabilities
−securities		+securities	+dealer loans	+dealer loans	
+deposits					+deposits

The balance sheets show how the preference shift can be accommodated, but not why it is in the interest of dealers and banks to do so. Presumably dealers will be willing to increase their holding of securities only if they can get a good (low) price, and banks will be willing to increase their holding of dealer loans only if they can get a good (high) rate. The size of the required price fluctuation presumably depends on the size of the portfolio shock that the dealer system is being asked to absorb, but, under the assumption that we are dealing with a small shock, a small fluctuation in price should be sufficient to bring forth the required accommodation. Such small accommodations are an everyday occurrence; market liquidity is sustained every day because funding liquidity is elastically forthcoming in this way.

How, if at all, will the Fed be involved in these everyday fluctuations? From the standpoint of the payments system, our hypothetical portfolio shock is nothing more than an unusual pattern of payments. In effect, wealth holders want their cash inflows to exceed cash outflows, and dealers are willing to accommodate them by allowing their own cash outflows to exceed cash inflows. In a single-big-bank system, this would be handled by a pair of book entries. In our decentralized payments system, however, there is a problem because households are unwilling to hold the kind of liabilities that dealers issue. The solution is to have the banking system accept the liabilities of the dealers, and to issue liabilities that households find more satisfactory. It follows that, to the extent that the Fed sees the portfolio shift as merely a fluctuation in the pattern of payments, it will accommodate the necessary expansion of bank credit by means of expansionary open market operations in the repo market. If the Fed is successful, then the federal funds rate will remain unchanged and banks may even be willing to absorb fluctuations in dealer borrowing at an unchanged spread over an unchanged federal funds rate.

What about the price of securities? If funding costs do not rise then dealers will not require quite as large a price discount as incentive to increase their holding of securities. But the degree of asset price movement will depend on what the assets are that the wealth holders are trying to exchange for money, and what the assets are that the Fed is willing to accept as collateral for its repo lending. At one extreme, we can imagine that wealth holders sell Treasury securities and the Fed lends against Treasury collateral, so the net effect is no change at all in any asset price; in effect, the Fed's repo lending absorbs the entire portfolio preference fluctuation. At the other extreme, we can imagine that wealth holders sell something more exotic, perhaps something for which no dealer makes a regular two-way market, and certainly something that the Fed does not accept as repo collateral. Then the effect on security prices will be large even if the Fed stabilizes the federal funds rate. The dealer system may still be able to accommodate the portfolio shift, but not without significant asset price fluctuation.

What accounts for the difference between the Treasury case and the exotic case? Many things, probably, but from the perspective of the money view, one thing stands out: liquidity. By hypothesis there is no dealer making a regular two-way market in the exotic security, and that means that the yield spread between the exotic security and Treasuries, a spread that might in good times be only a few basis points, will have to widen until a real-money investor is willing to take the other side of the trade. The important point is that even if the Fed ensures rather elastic *funding* liquidity, that does not necessarily translate into perfect *market* liquidity for all assets. Market liquidity will be highest for those assets that are immediately shiftable to the Fed because they are acceptable as collateral for borrowing. Other assets will be liquid only to the extent that some dealer finds it profitable to make a two-way market in them, and that can easily change over time, perhaps even suddenly. One day Lehman Brothers was making a two-way market in various derivatives of mortgage-backed securities, and the next day it wasn't.

Consider now the case of a *large* portfolio shift. Suppose that dealers do their thing, and banks do their thing, and the Fed does its thing, so the federal funds rate stays stable while bank credit and dealer balance sheets expand to absorb the shock. But security prices fall across the board, most sharply for the least liquid securities. Holders of those securities who mark their holdings to market are forced to recognize losses, and leveraged holders find their creditworthiness impaired. The survival constraint binds for them, and perhaps the solvency constraint as well. Failure of one such institution brings other institutions under suspicion, so everyone looks to contract the credit they are offering while hoarding any liquid reserves they may have. Money rates spike in the Eurodollar market, notwithstanding Fed intervention to stabilize the federal funds rate. Liquidity is like that. Here today, gone tomorrow.

The point is that, in a really severe crisis, market liquidity is no longer a matter of the funding liquidity of private dealers but rather of shiftability to the Fed. If an asset is not shiftable to the Fed, it may not be shiftable at all, or only at an unacceptably large price discount. The Fed in a crisis is not so much the lender of last resort (funding liquidity) as it is the dealer of last resort (market liquidity). If the dealers cannot or will not absorb the portfolio shift and the Fed continues to treat the portfolio shift as simply an unusual payments pattern, then the Fed's backstop of the payments system ultimately requires it to absorb the portfolio shift on its own balance sheet. Here is what such an extreme case might look like.

Wealth Holders		Fed		Banking System	
Assets	Liabilities	Assets	Liabilities	Assets	Liabilities
−securities		+securities	+reserves	+reserves	
+deposits					+deposits

Note that, in this hypothetical, the Fed is doing exactly what the dealer was doing in what I called a "normal crisis." It is borrowing from the banking system by expanding its reserve liabilities rather than dealer loans, but everything else is the same. Think of "securities" as "mortgage-backed securities" and you have a fairly accurate stylized picture of how balance sheets actually stand as of this writing (recall figure 1). It took a while to get there (see chap. 6) but get there we did. Under modern conditions, backstop of market liquidity requires the Fed to serve as dealer of last resort.

Monetary Policy

From the perspective of the classic money view, monetary policy was all about using "bank rate" to influence the balance of elasticity and discipline that is imposed by the survival constraint that faces each individual entity in the system. The idea was to intervene *before* the crisis in order to avoid later intervention of last resort.

In modern arrangements, the important policy rate is the federal funds rate. The Federal Reserve Board announces a specific target rate at regular intervals, and the open markets desk enforces that target by intervening daily in the repo market to absorb fluctuating demand. The federal funds rate is the modern analog to Bagehot's bank rate, but in modern discussion Bagehot's language of elasticity and discipline is largely gone, as is his focus on conditions in the money market. Today policymakers talk a language of economic stabilization and they focus attention on macroeconomic conditions, a shift in language and focus that remains as a legacy of the Age of Management.

It is not that modern policymakers are unconcerned with liquidity but rather that they have convinced themselves, or rather have been convinced by economists, that matters of liquidity (the purview of an antiquated money view) can be conceptually as well as operationally separated from matters of economic stabilization (the purview of the modern economics view). The present crisis has posed a rather decisive challenge to this neat division of intellectual labor, but inevitably past habits of thought persist and it is these habits that must be confronted if we are to learn the lessons that the crisis has to teach us.

Current macroeconomic thinking is organized around something called the dynamic stochastic general equilibrium (DSGE) model, which we can understand loosely as a jazzed-up version of the Walrasian equilibrium model that was at the center of the thinking of a previous generation. Time and risk are now explicitly modeled, but that is the only substantive change; abstraction from monetary plumbing remains of the essence, even more so today than in the past through the convenient analytical assumption of a so-called representative agent. (If there is only one agent, there can obviously be no private credit.) In some "New Keynesian" versions of the model, the kind of institutional rigidities and frictions that Tobin once emphasized are added on top of the basic DSGE, with rigidities separated into "nominal" and "real" subcategories; essentially all academic debate is about the empirical importance of these rigidities. It is not surprising, therefore, that the impulse of academic economists, faced with the crisis, has been to add a category of "financial" rigidities (and shocks) to the basic model; this program is well under way.[6]

Where this standard economics view confronts the money view most directly is on the question of how to set the federal funds rate, a question on which proponents of the economics view have developed a common stance that goes under the heading "Inflation Targeting." The idea is that the overriding purpose of monetary policy is long-run stabilization of the price level, and for that purpose the important thing is to signal credibly to the market that rising prices (perhaps even mere expectation of rising prices) will be met with firmly rising policy interest rates. Knowing this policy rule, market participants are supposed to form long-run expectations of a stable price level, expectations that then feed into their investment and consumption behavior in the short run. In that short run, rigidities and frictions may cause the economy to deviate a bit from the ideal, so the policy rule may want to deviate a bit as well, and that is what the academic debate is all about.

More or less all modern academic debate is organized as argument about the appropriate quantitative settings for a Taylor rule.[7] The underlying idea of the rule is that the market by itself tends to set the nominal interest rate equal to the natural rate plus expected inflation—this is the Fisher effect, named after Irving Fisher—but that is not enough to stabilize prices or income. The role of the Fed in stabilizing the long-run price level shows up in a parameter that describes how the Fed responds to deviations of inflation from the target. The role of the Fed in stabilizing employment shows up in a parameter that describes how the Fed responds to deviations from full employment. This construct is supposed to be an alternative to the old Keynesian and monetarist constructs, and as such it is supposed to replace Marschak-Tobin as the framework for policymakers to think about how to set the federal funds rate.

From a money view perspective, the important question is how an interest rate policy guided by a Taylor rule feeds into the behavior of the dealer system, the central institution that translates funding liquidity into market liquidity. So far in this chapter we have focused on the role of the Fed in stabilizing funding costs for the dealers and on the consequence of such stabilization for asset prices both in normal times and during crises. Now we extend the analysis to consider the role of the Fed in *changing* funding costs for the dealers. Translated into the language of the money view, the inflation targeting approach could be said to advocate leaning toward additional discipline when prices are rising faster than the inflation target, and leaning toward additional elasticity when prices are rising slower than the inflation target.

From the money view perspective, the most remarkable blind spot in the Taylor rule framework is the implication that interest rate policy should not take any notice of asset prices. The inherent instability of credit operates, after all, through a destabilizing feedback between expansion of credit and a rising market price of collateral. The money view does not tell us which asset prices to watch, since the dynamic can occur in commodities, financial assets, and even real assets such as land and houses; we've got to be watching them all. By contrast, the Taylor rule says we don't have to watch any of them; we only have to watch the index of consumer prices, which does not include any asset prices. That can be a problem.

In a money view perspective, if the Fed fails to raise interest rates in the face of a credit-fueled asset price bubble, the bubble will feed on itself, growing ever larger and having ever greater distorting effects, until it bursts. Concretely, if funding liquidity is too cheap, then market liquidity will be too cheap as well. The mechanism that connects the two is leverage on the dealer's balance sheet—too much leverage when funding liquidity is too cheap. Low funding rates thus support high asset prices, and particularly so in the case of assets that are not usually supported by a two-way dealer (such as residential housing). These are the assets that are most likely to become overvalued on the upside, and these are also the assets that are most likely to suffer the largest correction on the downside.

Why so? We have already seen how funding liquidity does not translate perfectly into market liquidity for any assets that are not immediately shiftable to the Fed, and especially not for any assets that lack the support of a two-way dealer. It follows that if funding costs are distorted by monetary policy, then a fortiori so will be asset prices; excess liquidity may have little effect on the price of assets that are already liquid, and most effect on the price of assets that are most illiquid. One way that effect is transmitted is through extension of two-way dealer support to new classes of assets during the boom.

It can all work fine for a while, as money markets do their job of channeling funds from those with excess cash inflow to those with excess cash outflow, while the Fed provides support for any necessary expansion of bank credit by stabilizing the effective federal funds rate. (In practice, in the run-up to the present crisis, the Eurodollar market and the repo market offered quite satisfactory sunny-day substitutes for expansion of federal funds credit.) The money view emphasizes the inherent instability of a credit system driven by the private profit motive, but the problem is made worse when the Fed adopts a policy rule that denies any responsibility for preventing a bubble. "As long as the music is playing, you've got to get up and dance," said Chuck Prince, then the CEO of Citibank, in July 2007.

The problem is that the music does not just stop, it switches into reverse. Suddenly, those with excess cash inflows want to hold cash assets, not loans, and those with excess cash outflows find themselves face-to-face with the survival constraint. Public funding liquidity may still be flowing at the center of the system, in the federal funds market, but it no longer translates into private market liquidity on the periphery. As market liquidity vanishes, collateral values crumble and private funding liquidity—both secured repo funding and unsecured Eurodollar funding—contracts. Sharp cuts in the federal funds rate may offer cheap public funding liquidity as a substitute but, as always, there are many slips between the funding liquidity cup and the market liquidity lip. In the end, it all comes down to the question of shiftability to the balance sheet of the central bank.

The simple point that has been made abundantly clear by the present crisis is that it is not at all easy to separate matters of liquidity from matters of economic stabilization; both conceptually and operationally they are intertwined. Abstracting from money may make our economic theory easier, but it does not make our economic policy better. At its core, our monetary system is a dealer system that supports the liquidity of our securities markets, and the Fed serves as dealer-in-chief not only in wartime but also in peacetime, and especially in financial crisis time. The sooner we confront this institutional reality, the better we will be able to face the reconstruction that lies ahead.

SIX

Learning from the Crisis

From the perspective of the money view, the financial crisis that began in August 2007 and then took a sharp turn for the worse in September 2008 looks like a stress test of the brave new world of modern finance that we have been building ever since about 1970. First currency swaps, then interest rate swaps, and then credit default swaps were introduced, and the eventual result was transformation of the rigid and highly regulated financial system that we had inherited from Depression-era reform. Regulatory arbitrage was not the only driver of this transformation but the important thing is the consequence, a capital-market-based credit system that is now a more important source of credit than the traditional banking system. I take it as given that this brave new world is here to stay, modulo a certain amount of tinkering. What does the crisis have to teach us about the kind of tinkering that may be necessary?

Tinkering may be a bad choice of words, since it suggests that not much needs to be done, but I choose it advisedly because I take it to be the lesson of history that any new system must grow organically out of the old one. We are not going to start from scratch, so our reforms had better engage with the system as it is, not as it was or as we might wish it to be in some ideal world. As always, the main obstacle to change is the lag of thinking behind experience. In this respect, the great positive contribution of the crisis has been to make that lag evident, and thus to open our minds to the possibility of new ways of understanding the system that has grown up in front of our eyes.

A rehabilitation of the nineteenth-century money view is, I have suggested, the place to start, but it is not the place to end. The concept of liquidity that seemed appropriate for Bagehot is no longer appropriate for us. Long ago we switched over from Bagehot's emphasis on the "self-liquidating" character of certain short-term commercial debts to more appropriate emphasis on the "shiftability" of certain securities in liquid markets. But we have not yet switched over from Bagehot's conception of the central bank as "lender of last resort" to the more appropriate modern conception of it as "dealer of last resort." The most important contribution of the crisis has been to force us to make that conceptual leap in practice, as a practical response to the exigencies of the crisis. The job now is for theory to follow practice, reconstructing the money view for modern times.

In historical retrospect, McChesney Martin's 1952 policy of "bills only" established the institutional foundations for our modern system by setting the division of labor between the Fed and the private dealer system. In Martin's vision, the Fed would provide funding liquidity through its support for the money market, and the dealer system would translate that funding liquidity into market liquidity in support of the longer-term capital market. This vision proved prescient. In 1952, Martin's main concern was about leaving to the private dealers the market for long-term Treasury bonds. But as private capital markets recovered and grew, the same division of labor was extended to corporate bonds and then, with some help from Fannie Mae and Freddie Mac, to household mortgage bonds as well. At the peak in 2006, household debt (mostly mortgage debt) accounted for 44.3 percent of outstanding nonfinancial debt in the United States, compared to 32.1 percent corporate debt and only 23.6 percent government debt.[1]

Even as the financial system evolved, the overarching vision of how the division of labor was supposed to work remained the same. The Fed intervened in the market for Treasury repo with the goal of stabilizing the federal funds rate at some target, and that was all. Other repo rates and the Eurodollar rate got stabilized through money market arbitrage by private dealers, and the private money market then served as the source of funding liquidity for dealer operations in securities of all kinds, producing the two-way dealer markets that are the source of market liquidity. Monetary management was largely limited to manipulation of the federal funds rate. A change in the funds rate affected market liquidity and thus asset prices by affecting other money rates and funding liquidity. That is how Martin thought the system should work, and how in fact it eventually did work, until it stopped working in August 2007.

Martin's vision was based, as we have seen, on historical American practice that had been highlighted by Harold Moulton as early as 1918, practice that predated the establishment of the Fed and that Moulton hoped the Fed would find a way to support rather than to replace, all in the interest of the capital development of the nation. Depression and war interrupted the evolutionary trajectory from those early days, but only temporarily. From a long historical point of view, the central lesson of the crisis is that the American system requires the Fed's support as dealer of last resort, not just in the money market (as emphasized by Martin) but also in the capital market, and not just for Treasury securities (as emphasized by Martin) but also for private securities. The practical intertwining of money markets and capital markets is the defining institutional feature of the American system, and that feature requires a similarly integrated backstop by the central bank.

It is the Fed's acceptance of its role as dealer of last resort that finally put a floor under the crisis, as I will argue in detail later in this chapter, but that leaves open the question, what next? In this regard, it is worth recalling that, once the Bank of England recognized its role as lender of last resort, the logical next step was to find ways to avoid ever getting to that last resort; this has been the goal of monetary policy and of financial regulation ever since. By analogy, now that the Fed has recognized its role as dealer of last resort, the next step will be to use that new awareness as the foundation for development of a new generation of monetary policy and financial regulation. The crisis marks the beginning of that process, but meanwhile old patterns of thought stand in the way.

The Long Shadow of Jimmy Stewart

From a money view perspective, the so-called shadow banking system was only one part of a larger integrated system in which funding liquidity in the money market was translated into market liquidity in the capital market. But that is not how matters looked to most people. The very term *shadow bank* reveals how the new market-based credit system was viewed initially (and still is viewed) from the perspective of the traditional bank-based credit system.

In partial defense of that popular view, it is certainly true that the new system emerged out of the traditional system, and also relied symbiotically—some might say parasitically—on ties with that system. Moreover, those ties turned out to be crucial during the crisis, since, when the shadow banking system collapsed, it collapsed first onto the traditional banking system. Only when the resulting load proved too heavy for the traditional banking system to bear did the system of government backstops come into play, a system of backstops that had never been intended to support the market-based system.

Thus the government wound up supporting the new system indirectly and unintentionally, rather than directly and on purpose. Instead of putting a floor under the new market-based credit system, the government has been intervening to prop up and restore the old bank-based credit system. One consequence has been to raise the prospect that the market-based system might have been nothing more than a temporary aberration, and that it might be possible (even desirable) to roll back history to an earlier and simpler time. This is wishful nostalgia for a world that never was, nostalgia for the Jimmy Stewart banking of blessed holiday memory; but nostalgia is a powerful force and we neglect its influence on our thinking at our peril.

In traditional banking, so nostalgic memory reminds us, banks took deposits from households in their community and made loans to other households in their community. It was a simple business, and its main risks were solvency risk and liquidity risk. Solvency risk was about the prospect of loan default, and it was handled by a buffer of bank capital, backstopped by deposit insurance at the FDIC. Liquidity risk was about the prospect of deposit withdrawals, and it was handled by a buffer of cash reserves, backstopped by the discount window at the Fed. This is the model of banking that was in the back of most of our minds as we looked at the new shadow banking system, and from this vantage point it seemed clear that the new system involved exposure to familiar solvency and liquidity risks, but those familiar exposures were handled differently. To make the analogy with traditional banking clear, I show the two stylized balance sheets side by side below.

From a Jimmy Stewart perspective, the central feature of shadow banking involved a financial institution holding securitized loans (rather than whole loans) and funding those loans in the wholesale money market (rather than with retail deposits). In the shadow banking system, solvency risk was handled not so much by means of capital buffers as by means of insurance of various kinds, which I show as the purchase of a credit default swap (CDS). And liquidity risk was handled not so much by means of cash reserves as by using the securitized loans as collateral for borrowing in the wholesale money market. I show this borrowing as asset-backed commercial paper (ABCP) and repo (RP), instruments typically held as investments by an institutional money market mutual fund (not shown).[2] The important thing is that in the shadow banking system neither solvency risk nor liquidity risk was backstopped in any direct way by the government. Shadow banking was Jimmy Stewart banking without the regulation, but also without the protection.

Traditional Bank		*Shadow Bank*	
Assets	Liabilities	Assets	Liabilities
cash reserves	deposits	securitized loans	money market funding
loans	capital buffer	CDS	—ABCP
			—RP

Was that a bad thing? It could be argued (and indeed was argued) that so long as the government is not on the hook as backstop, there is no great need for regulation. Widows and orphans are presumably not holding ABCP and RP, so maybe we can dispense with deposit insurance (and the resulting moral hazard). Furthermore, ABCP and RP are not part of the money supply, so maybe there is no macroeconomic reason to worry either and we can dispense with reserve requirements as well. In retrospect, the premises of both conclusions were faulty, but the important point to appreciate is how their acceptance was shaped by the Jimmy Stewart conception of banking.

The same distorting perspective has shaped our understanding of the subsequent collapse. In the early days of the crisis, it seemed to be nothing more than a classic bank run playing itself out among the unregulated shadow banks rather than the regulated traditional banks, involving annoying disruption of the wholesale money market rather than dread contraction of retail bank deposits and the money supply. Since one role of deposit insurance is to prevent bank runs, it was not really surprising that the uninsured shadow banking system turned out to be vulnerable to runs. All it took for the money market mutual fund holders of ABCP and RP to take flight was the slightest anxiety about the value of the collateral that was supposed to be securing their loans. Thus, so the story goes, as a result of nothing more than initial anxiety, shadow banks found themselves unable to roll over their money market funding; the typical consequence was to trigger backup liquidity support from some parent entity, which was usually a bank.[3]

The first market to collapse was ABCP, in fall 2007. But expansion of RP funding took up much of the slack, and expansion of unsecured borrowing by shadow bank parents took up the rest. (In unsecured borrowing the balance sheet of the borrower is the security, instead of some specific financial instrument.) Rates spiked in Eurodollar and financial commercial paper (CP) markets to attract the needed funding, but the funding got done. The holders of ABCP were worried about the underlying collateral, but the parents of the shadow banks apparently were not (yet), since they were willing to take it back onto their own balance sheets; and the market was not worried about the parents (yet), since it was willing to lend to them. Thus, in the first stage of the crisis, the traditional banking system was willing and able to act as private lender of last resort to the shadow banking system.

Meanwhile, the Fed served dutifully as lender of last resort to the traditional banking system. Like the parents of the shadow banks, the Fed professed not to be worried about the quality of the collateral, and made room for some of it at the discount window by relaxing collateral requirements and by expanding eligibility requirements. The Term Auction Facility (TAF), introduced in December 2007, was the most important funding channel, serving as an anonymous discount window where banks could bid for funds, for terms up to ninety days. The Fed funded its lending by selling Treasury bills, in effect offering Treasury bills as a substitute for the ABCP that the market no longer wanted. Thus, all those who shunned ABCP got offered their pick of alternative money market assets: RP, financial CP, and also (for those who were very afraid) Treasury bills. And for a while it seemed to be working.

But then, in March 2008, Bear Stearns collapsed and the crisis entered a new phase. Now it was the RP market that collapsed, as haircuts demanded by lenders soared.[4] Lenders were focusing, it seems, not on the fundamental value of the collateral but rather on its likely sale price in disordered markets. Even so, unsecured borrowing markets were able to take up most of the slack, again backstopped by the Fed, which now extended lender of last resort support directly to dealers through a new Primary Dealer Credit Facility (PDCF), and also through the Term Securities Lending Facility (TSLF) which lent Treasuries against non-Treasury collateral that was no longer acceptable for private repo. Again it seemed to be working. Eurodollar rates stabilized at a high spread over federal funds rates; the Fed was lending freely and the marginal borrower was paying a high rate, just as Bagehot recommended.

Finally, in September 2008, with the collapse of Lehman Brothers and then AIG, even unsecured money market funding froze up. Indeed, even the Treasury RP market froze as everyone preferred to hold on to Treasury collateral; when the music stops you want the government to be your counterparty. Throughout the system, everyone faced the problem of finding dollar money market funding, but the problem was most acute for those who did not have access to the Fed. The resulting scramble for funding drove LIBOR rates to unprecedented spreads over federal funds rates, and the Fed responded by extending lender of last resort even further, accepting a wider selection of collateral from a wider selection of counterparties.

One major category of necessitous borrower was everyone who depended on commercial paper borrowing for funding, which meant nonfinancial borrowers as well as financial borrowers. To handle this problem, the Fed created the Commercial Paper Funding Facility, which used the Fed's balance sheet to lend directly to such needy borrowers.[5] Another major category of necessitous borrower was the many foreign banks that had been forced to absorb their own shadow banks, and therefore now faced the problem of rolling their dollar money market funding. To handle this problem, the Fed used its liquidity swap line with foreign central banks, a program that in its essentials amounted to an extension of discount window borrowing to foreign banks, but with foreign central banks as intermediary taking all the credit risk.[6]

From a Jimmy Stewart perspective, this final expansion of the Fed's role, dramatic though it was, seemed to be nothing more than an extension of traditional lender of last resort support. The only difference was the scale of the lending, which meant that the Fed could no longer fund its lending simply by liquidating its holding of Treasury bills. Now it had to expand its liabilities as well, mainly by borrowing from member banks (paying interest on reserves for the first time), and by borrowing from the Treasury to make up any funding difference.

The Jimmy Stewart perspective can be summarized in the following series of balance sheets. The first set shows how the shadow banking system funded itself before the crisis, mainly by issuing money market securities that were purchased by money market mutual funds. The second set shows how the shadow bank parents stepped in when secured funding dried up because of concern about collateral values. The third set shows how the Fed stepped in to support the shadow bank parents when unsecured funding also dried up. From a Jimmy Stewart perspective, these balance sheets tell a story of lender of last resort, first private and then public.

Funding the Shadow Banking System

Shadow Bank		Money Market Mutual Fund	
Assets	Liabilities	Assets	Liabilities
securitized loans	ABCP	ABCP	"deposits"
CDS	RP	RP	

Private Lender of Last Resort

Shadow Bank Parent		Money Market Mutual Fund	
Assets	Liabilities	Assets	Liabilities
securitized loans	Eurodollar deposit	Eurodollar deposit	"deposits"
CDS	financial CP	financial CP	

Public Lender of Last Resort

Shadow Bank Parent		Fed	
Assets	Liabilities	Assets	Liabilities
securitized loans	TAF loan	TAF loan	currency
CDS	PDCF loan	PDCF loan	bank reserves
	liquidity swap	liquidity swap	Treasury deposits

From a broader money view perspective, however, September 2008 was the moment when the Fed moved from lender of last resort to dealer of last resort, in effect taking the collapsing wholesale money market onto its own balance sheet. But in the heat of the moment, no one noticed. At the very moment when the Fed's balance sheet was doubling in size, public attention was instead diverted from the problem of liquidity to the problem of solvency, focused in that direction by the Treasury's request for a $700 billion Congressional authorization to buy troubled assets. Later the Treasury's strategy would morph into a plan to recapitalize the banks, but the important point to emphasize is how the Jimmy Stewart paradigm shaped the immediate policy response. When liquidity risk was thought to be the issue, it was the Fed's problem; when solvency risk was thought to be the issue, it became the Treasury's problem. In both respects, the fact that the shadow banking system had collapsed onto the traditional banking system made it seem as though the problem was now just a traditional banking problem. The problem became how to save the banking system—a big problem, to be sure, but at least a comfortably familiar problem intellectually.

A Stress Test of Moulton-Martin

Unfortunately, within this intellectual comfort zone it was impossible to confront the central question posed by the crisis: why did the shadow banks collapse in the first place? Indeed, it is not just the shadow banks but, more important, the larger capital-market-based credit system that failed, and it is that failure that we must understand if we are to put the system back together again, and on more solid foundations this time. This financial crisis is not merely a subprime mortgage crisis or even a shadow banking crisis; it is a crisis of the entire market-based credit system that we have constructed since 1970, following Martin's 1952 report and Moulton (1918).

From this standpoint, what immediately draws attention is the utter breakdown of the underlying system of funding liquidity. This is the plumbing behind the walls, and it failed very dramatically. Before the crisis, almost all funding of the shadow banks was supplied by private lending in both secured and unsecured money markets. From this point of view, the successive breakdown of ABCP, then RP, and then the financial CP markets was not just about the shadow banks not being able to borrow, but also and more fundamentally about a breakdown in the dealer system that had ensured liquidity in those wholesale money markets.

The big thing that happened in September 2008 was that the system of private dealer money market arbitrage, having been under stress for more than a year, finally froze up completely. And the big thing about the Fed's response was that it stepped in as the dealer of last resort to replace the private dealer system. Banks that needed funds borrowed from the Fed through the discount window, while banks with surplus funds lent them to the Fed by holding excess reserve balances. Banks that were short of collateral eligible for discount borrowed instead directly through the new commercial paper facility or the liquidity swap facility, and money market mutual funds that could not deposit at the Fed instead bought Treasury bills and the Treasury deposited the proceeds at the Fed.

The contemporaneous economists' debate about the expansion of the Fed's balance sheet largely missed this most important point. Bernanke and his supporters talked about credit easing (Fed lending) while his critics talked about quantitative easing (Fed borrowing that expanded the reserve base), so reprising a largely irrelevant precrisis debate about the relative importance of the "credit channel" and the "money channel" in the transmission of monetary policy. Meanwhile, the fact that the Fed's balance sheet had expanded on *both* sides tells us that something else was going on. The Fed was moving the wholesale money market onto its own balance sheet, stepping in as dealer of last resort for the money market. (In September 2008, it was yet unwilling to go the next step to serve as dealer of last resort in the capital market, but that would come soon enough.)

Once we think about the Fed's balance sheet expansion in this way, the doubling seems in fact rather small. After all, the wholesale money market is much larger than the mere trillion or so that the Fed took on. But the reason the Fed did not have to do even more than that was that, by acting as dealer of last resort, the Fed operated also to support continued lending in the private money market, which would otherwise have frozen. In effect, the Fed was offering standing facilities, both buying and selling money, at prices away from market prices so only those who most needed it took advantage. Simply knowing that the Fed was there as a backstop made others willing to deal privately inside the Fed's bid-ask spread.

But why did private funding liquidity disappear in the first place? The sequential character of the collapse makes clear that the underlying problem was with the collateral, first the explicit collateral in the form of securities used for secured money market funding, and then the implicit collateral in the form of balance sheet net worth used for unsecured money market funding. When collateral valuations came under threat, so too did the ability to use that collateral to raise funding. But why did collateral valuations come under threat? Fundamental valuation was definitely a concern—bad loans had definitely been made—but from a money view perspective, price is first of all a matter of market liquidity, and this perspective focuses attention on the dealer system that translated funding liquidity into market liquidity.

From the very beginning, the shadow banking system was completely dependent on a well-functioning dealer system in two senses. First, the dealer system determined the security prices (market liquidity) that established the value of collateral. Second, the dealer system determined the price and availability (funding liquidity) of the money that could be raised using that collateral. In both capital markets and money markets, dealers quoted prices and allowed their balance sheets to absorb the resulting order flow, both buying and selling. From this perspective, the shadow banking system was a source of order flow, a demander of liquidity that the private dealer system supplied.

To understand how this worked, and therefore how it broke, it is helpful to situate the shadow banks more precisely within the larger financial system. The place to start is to recognize that the shadow banks were holding (and funding) only the very highest-rated tranches created by a larger securitization process that packaged loans and then sliced and diced the package into securities with specifically tailored risk characteristics. Riskier tranches were held—indeed, were designed to be held—by pension funds, insurance companies, and hedge funds. By contrast to the shadow banks, these other institutions each funded their own slice with their own characteristic liabilities, *not* with money market funding.[7] They were, thus, not demanders of funding liquidity. But they were demanders of market liquidity, at least potentially, since they depended on the shiftability of their asset holdings to limit their risk exposure.

The source of that market liquidity was not, however, in the market for the assets themselves. The underlying securitization tranches were designed to be held, not traded, and in general they *were* held, not traded, and here is the source of a persistent challenge for the market-based credit system. If there is no trading, then where are the prices supposed to come from? And if there are no market prices, how are we supposed to reassure an ABCP or RP lender that the collateral supporting its short-term money loan is adequate?[8] In principle, we could give the lender explicit recourse to the balance sheet of the parent entity—that was the solution found when the crisis first struck—but the whole point of the system was to avoid such explicit recourse in order to avoid the regulatory restrictions that constrained the parent. So where did the prices come from?

In retrospect, it is clear that the source of market liquidity, and hence price, was in the market for credit *insurance* on the assets, or on assets of similar risk. The key to the whole thing was the credit default swap market, and the key supplier of market liquidity for credit default swaps was the investment banks, especially the investment banks that put together the original securitization deals. When the system was working, investment banks stood ready to make two-way markets in CDSs on securitization tranches that they had sold to clients. That was the source of market liquidity for the entire system, and that was the source of the prices used to value the underlying assets. When the investment banks ran into trouble and therefore pulled back from their market-making activity, market liquidity contracted and prices slumped. That explains why the collapse of Bear Stearns in March 2008, and then Lehman Brothers in September 2008, were such body blows for the market-based credit system. They were both moments of stepwise contraction of market liquidity.

But why did the investment banks get into trouble? To the extent that they were acting *strictly* as dealers, they would have tried to maintain a matched book, in which purchases of protection from some clients served to hedge sales of protection to other clients. One way that investment bank dealers did this was by packaging up credit risk in a so-called synthetic CDO (collateralized debt obligation) and selling it to a client. In a cash CDO, the credit risk exposure comes from owning a basket of underlying actual securities; in a synthetic CDO, the credit risk comes from selling credit protection on a basket of underlying securities. During the boom, when clients were beating down the doors for product, it was a relatively easy matter to sell such synthetic CDOs and, as a consequence, it was relatively easy for the investment bank dealers to achieve matched book.[9]

Another way they achieved matched book was by buying insurance on the upper tranches while selling insurance on the lower tranches. In doing so, however, they faced the problem of basis risk. When you sell protection on one asset and buy protection on another, you are depending on correlation between the two asset prices, and that correlation implies a hedging ratio. For example, suppose you sell protection on the BB tranche and buy protection on the AAA tranche, and you know that insurance on the AAA tranche moves $1 whenever insurance on the BB tranche moves $10. Then you need ten AAA contracts to hedge a single BB contract. That's a lot of AAA contracts, and it explains why problems with the AAA tranche were so devastating for the system as a whole.

If both the shadow banking system and the investment bank dealer system were net buyers of AAA protection, then who was the net seller? The answer, as we learned in the crisis, was the insurance industry, including traditional bond insurers such as Ambac and MBIA, but also new entities such as the Financial Products Division of AIG. By insuring only the AAA tranches, they convinced themselves that they were getting money for nothing, since their models told them that the insured risk was extremely improbable. And yet, their willingness to provide AAA protection was completely essential to the system; without it, dealers would not have been able to square up their CDS books and, hence, would not have been able to provide the market liquidity on which the entire system depended. The insurers were getting money for something, but without realizing what that something was.

The stylized balance sheets below show how the system worked, when it worked. Investment banks were the source of market liquidity, as they were prepared both to buy and to sell CDSs. Although no doubt they were also speculating, I treat them strictly as dealers, choosing their bid-ask prices in an attempt to achieve matched book; this treatment makes clear how the sine qua non of the system was the dealers' ability to buy AAA protection from the insurance industry.[10] The typical insurance company persuaded itself that by selling high-tranche insurance it was getting money for nothing. The typical investment bank persuaded itself that by buying sufficient high-tranche insurance it was achieving matched book. Both were proved wrong by subsequent events.

Investment Banks		Insurance Companies	
Assets	Liabilities	Assets	Liabilities
high-tranche CDSs	mid-tranche CDSs		high-tranche CDSs
	low-tranche CDSs		

This way of understanding how the system worked when it was working helps to explain one of the deepest puzzles about the boom that preceded the present crisis, namely, the extremely low credit spreads throughout the market. Everyone knew that someone was selling very cheap credit insurance, but everyone thought it was someone else. In the crisis we found out that the net seller was both the investment banks and the insurance companies. And the key mistake that both of them made was in not appreciating the liquidity dimension of the system.

From a money view perspective, the investment banks and the insurance companies were acting as suppliers of market liquidity. The insurers thought they were insuring a low-probability risk, whereas in fact they were acting as a private dealer of last resort, selling market liquidity and at a price that proved to be too generous. The dealers thought they had matched books, whereas in fact they were spreading the market liquidity in the high tranches into the lower tranches, taking on liquidity risk of their own. It all worked fine so long as the music was playing. On the way up, ample funding liquidity in private money markets supported the extension of market liquidity into previously uncharted territory, and that extension supported collateral valuations that supported further extension of funding liquidity. On the way down, the same reinforcing cycle worked in reverse. This is the inherent instability of credit, twenty-first-century edition.

From this point of view, the fundamental problem was that the insurance companies were writing contracts that they never should have been permitted to write. Like lender of last resort, dealer of last resort is inherently a public function, not a private function. Dealers thought they were taking no risk because they were calibrating their models using historical asset prices. In fact, however, their willingness to write those insurance contracts was changing the world, enabling great pockets of leverage to build up that would pose a problem of systemic risk that would overwhelm their private risk-bearing capacity. When AIG stopped writing these contracts, the game was over. Market liquidity drained from the system, and the entire self-reinforcing cycle began to work in reverse.

We can read that downward spiral in the chart of the AAA tranche of the ABX index, an index of the price of the top tranches of CDOs holding subprime mortgages (figure 2). The AAA rating refers to the rating of the underlying components of the index at the time of inception (2006 and 2007 vintages). Obviously, many of the underlying components have subsequently been very substantially downgraded. The important point is that in July 2007,

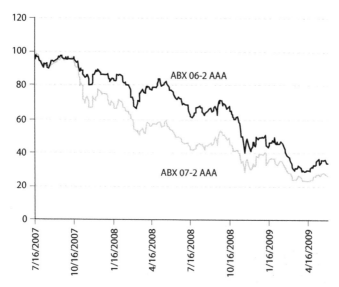

Figure 2: The price of mortgage-backed security collateral. Source: Markit

where the chart begins, the kind of liquidity effects that I have been describing probably conspired to drive prices *above* values. AAA tranches of CDOs backed by subprime mortgages were being valued as if they were Treasury securities.

Then, when crisis came, the same liquidity effects conspired to drive prices *below* values. As the crisis deepened, fundamental values also fell, of course, causing further contraction of market liquidity and driving prices down even further. But at the center of the downward spiral was a collapse of the private dealer system that translated funding liquidity into market liquidity. At the center of policy response to the crisis was the Fed, which stepped in as public dealer of last resort to backstop the collapsing private dealer system.

Dealer of Last Resort

In the initial phase of the crisis, as we have seen, the Fed focused its intervention on funding liquidity, depending on the private dealer system to translate that funding liquidity into market liquidity. That would have been enough in a "normal crisis," but this was no normal crisis. As the initial policy response proved insufficient, the Fed began to pay more attention to the market liquidity dimension directly.

We can date the beginning of that attention to the introduction, after the collapse of Bear Stearns in March 2008, of the new Term Securities Lending Facility. The TSLF offered to swap bona fide Treasury securities for private-label mortgage-backed securities (MBSs). Using this facility, any shadow bank parent that found itself holding an MBS that it could not repo, could swap that MBS for a Treasury bond that it could repo. (Initially, the facility was limited to MBSs rated AAA.) Legally, the swap was structured as a loan, but the risk exposure was that of a credit default swap, and the standing character of the facility meant that the Fed was in effect putting a ceiling on the price of one particular kind of credit protection insurance, and hence a floor under the price of the underlying referenced security.[11] The Fed was beginning to do, in its own small way, what AIG had been doing in a much bigger way. It was beginning to act as dealer of last resort to the capital market.

In retrospect, this early operation was a careful toe testing the waters in which the Fed, and the government more generally, would soon be paddling desperately. On September 7, 2008, the Treasury put Fannie Mae and Freddie Mac into conservatorship, in effect swapping Treasury debt for the debt of Fannie and Freddie. And then, on September 16, the Fed took over AIG's book of credit derivatives in exchange for an 80 percent equity stake in the company. Thus the government acquired the CDS portfolio that had been supporting the entire system; subsequently it acted to ensure performance of existing contracts, but not yet to write new ones.[12]

Various facilities to write new CDS contracts, or their economic equivalents, were soon forthcoming, however.[13] On October 21, a new Money Market Investor Funding Facility was announced, under which the Fed essentially provided a price floor at 90 percent of amortized cost for highly rated money market assets held by money market mutual funds.[14] There were no takers because expansion of deposit insurance to money market mutual fund accounts had already stopped the run, but this early facility seems to have provided the model for later facilities. In November 2008, in cooperation with the FDIC and the Treasury, the Fed wrote tail credit risk insurance on a collection of $306 billion of mortgage-related assets owned by Citigroup, followed by a similar deal for $138 billion of assets held by Bank of America. But both of these were one-off deals to handle problems faced by particularly troubled institutions.

Most significant, in an explicit effort to restart the securitization apparatus, in March 2009 the Fed opened the Term Asset-Backed Securities Loan Facility (TALF) to support the AAA tranches of new securitized lending.[15] The idea was to start with consumer loans (such as credit card receivables and auto loans) and then to move on to mortgage-backed securities, to start with newly issued securities and then to move on to legacy securities for which the market was frozen. Because the Fed's charter gives it lending authority, not insurance authority, the facility was structured as a loan. In fact, however, by lending ninety cents on the dollar on a nonrecourse basis at a rate of 100 basis points over LIBOR, the Fed was doing essentially what Lehman and AIG used to do, but with less leverage and charging a higher price. (The credit risk involved in such lending was covered by funds allocated from the Treasury's Troubled Asset Relief Program under section 102, "Insurance of Troubled Assets.")

Thus did the Fed expand its dealer of last resort intervention from the money market to the capital market. Operating as dealer of last resort, the Fed found itself inventing a new version of the Bagehot principle to guide its operations: *insure freely but at a high premium.* As dealer of last resort, what the Fed was insuring, it is important to emphasize, was not the payments that the debtor had promised to make but rather the market value of the promise itself; that is the difference between dealer of last resort and credit insurer of last resort. As in the original Bagehot principle, the idea is for the Fed to charge a price that provides incentive for the private market to undercut the Fed once it recovers.

So far, it seems to have worked according to plan, as a number of consumer asset-backed securitization deals have come to successful fruition through TALF, while others have come to successful fruition outside of TALF. The goal was to restart securitization, and that is what has been achieved. The scale of the program has, however, been much smaller than was anticipated at the launch and the reason for that seems to be that the details for expanding TALF to include mortgage-backed securities never got fully worked out.

Instead, the Fed has embarked on a separate program of *directly* purchasing mortgage-backed securities that are backed by one or another of the government-sponsored enterprises (GSEs) such as Fannie Mae and Freddie Mac. To date the Fed has accumulated more than $1 trillion of such securities, doing so by posting a bid price that is higher than the market. The Fed has been acting as dealer of last resort, not just in the credit insurance market, which was the source of market liquidity precrisis, but now in the capital market directly.

These are bold and innovative experiments, but the basic pattern comes through clearly. The Fed now recognizes that, for our market-based credit system, it must remake itself as dealer of last resort. The various facilities that the Fed has launched have been cobbled together in order to fit under existing legislative authority; in the longer run, legislation can be expected to adapt to the new reality. More fundamentally, we can look forward to a remake of the framework for monetary policy, going beyond the precrisis fixation on tracking the "natural" rate of interest, and taking account for the first time of the key connection to asset prices that runs from funding liquidity to market liquidity.

Conclusion

On the eve of the Fed's centennial year, we find ourselves grappling with many of the same issues that concerned the Fed's founders, albeit now with the benefit of a century's experience with central banking American style. To be sure, we have our own intellectual blinders to overcome, mainly a legacy of what I have called the Age of Management, but they are different blinders from those that held back our forebears. Unlike them, we are in a position to appreciate Moulton's emphasis on shiftability, as well as Martin's emphasis on the dealer system as the source of that shiftability. Our blinders involve, if anything, *excessive* appreciation of these emphases and insufficient appreciation of their limitations. To say that the essence of liquidity is shiftability is not to say that liquidity is or should be a free good, and it is not to say that we can safely abstract from liquidity when we consider questions of monetary policy and financial regulation. This is the central lesson of the crisis.

What are the implications of the Fed's new role as "dealer of last resort" for normal times? That is the question that we must confront looking forward, starting from the realization that our market-based credit system relies critically on two-way dealer markets that link funding liquidity in the money market with market liquidity in the capital market. The Fed must think of its role as intervening to support and manage that system as a whole, not just to set the price in a narrow slice of the funding markets.

In the money market, the Fed's responsibilities clearly must involve ongoing oversight of private *funding liquidity*, in RP and Eurodollar markets as well as federal funds, since the Fed inevitably serves as dealer of last resort to these wholesale money markets. This is new, but arguably a straightforward extension of Bagehot.

What is not a straightforward extension of Bagehot is the Fed's likely ongoing concern with *market liquidity*, and not just in Treasury securities but also in private securities, most importantly mortgage-backed securities. A key lesson of the crisis is that funding liquidity is not enough, since in a crisis funding liquidity does not get translated into market liquidity, no matter how hard the Fed works to push funds out the door. As dealer of last resort, the goal of the Fed should not be to set the market price but only to set a price floor, which in normal times should be some distance away from the market price.

To fix ideas, consider the stylized balance sheet below, which shows the private dealer system engaged in harvesting one liquidity premium in the term structure of interest rates (first line), and also another liquidity premium in the credit structure of interest rates (second line), in both cases financing its positions in the repo market (third line). This is a straightforward extension of the stylized dealer treated in chapter 5. The only difference is that here I am concerned about market liquidity, not funding liquidity. The behavior of the private dealer system is driven by the tradeoff between expected profit and risk.

Private Dealer System

Assets	Liabilities
Treasury bonds	Treasury bills
mortgage-backed securities	Treasury bonds
RP lending	RP borrowing

The job of the Fed is not to eliminate the risk that dealers face but rather to put bounds on it, to establish an arena within which private calculation of expected profit and risk makes sense. Since risk is not eliminated, neither is expected profit; liquidity is not a free good. We should therefore expect the term structure arbitrage to make money on average, but that is because it is risky; the same goes for the credit structure arbitrage. The goal of the Fed should not be to get as close as possible to the impossible ideal of perfect liquidity, but only to set bounds that keep the system from running off the rails.

For this purpose, it is helpful to think of the dealer of last resort function as a kind of tail risk insurance. For example, think of the Fed as standing ready always to buy some select group of AAA private securities at eighty cents on the dollar; this is a kind of limit order, an out-of-the-money trading option, but it can also be viewed as a kind of credit protection that insures the price of the referenced security will never fall below eighty. The twenty-cent haircut is there to serve the same function that the high interest rate does in classic lender of last resort intervention: it ensures that those who use the facility do so only as a last resort.

In practice, during normal times, probably no one will use the facility at all; the Fed wants to bear tail *liquidity* risk, not tail *credit* risk, and in order to avoid the latter, its dealer of last resort price may have to be set rather far from the market price. Some other arm of government, *not* the Fed, may be required to bear tail credit risk in order to establish somewhat tighter bounds within which private dealers can reasonably be expected to operate. (In just this way, the Treasury has taken on the credit risk involved in the Fed's TALF program and the GSEs have taken on the credit risk in the Fed's MBS purchase program.) But there is an important difference between a credit insurer of last resort and a dealer of last resort; for the latter, the goal is guaranteeing shiftability, not indemnifying for losses of wealth. This conceptual distinction has been characteristic of all of the Fed's interventions during the crisis, and it seems to be a model that could work in normal times as well.

Having set the bounds that establish the possibility of rational risk calculation, the Fed can then turn its attention to its more traditional function, setting the money rate of interest. It will, however, no longer be possible to maintain the illusion that monetary policy is about macroeconomic management, separate from liquidity management. The Fed has *two* instruments and *two* targets, but both instruments influence both targets and must be considered together. The details of how exactly this would work can be left for future work. Here, it must suffice to observe that pushing around the money rate of interest inevitably pushes around the expected profit from term structure and credit structure arbitrage, and hence the willingness of the dealer system to expand, thus supporting market liquidity and hence asset prices.

The classic money view urged central bankers to attend to the balance of discipline and elasticity in the money market, in order to manage the inherent instability of credit. Our modern world is not Bagehot's world, by a long shot, but at the highest level of abstraction the classic money view holds as true in our world as in his. The money market is where promises made are measured against results achieved, and committed cash outflows are weighed against realized cash inflows. The survival constraint is the discipline that maintains the coherence of our decentralized market system, and management of that constraint is the most important duty of the central bank.

Notes

Introduction

1. Shiller (2008), Morris (2008), Zandi (2009).
2. Wicksell (1936 [1898]).
3. Woodford (2003).
4. Taylor (2009).

Chapter One: Lombard Street, Old and New

1. Minsky (1967, 33).
2. Hawtrey (1923).
3. Schumpeter (1934). There is, of course, also risk on the other side—risk of fostering excessive growth on the way up and excessive destruction on the way down. This is the risk emphasized by modern neo-Austrian writers such as Claudio Borio and William White (2004).
4. Hawtrey (1934).
5. General collateral repo typically pays a higher interest rate than Treasury repo, but both rates are typically lower than the federal funds rate. Quoted Eurodollar rates are typically higher than federal funds rates, but usually by only a few basis points.
6. Brunnermeier and Pedersen (2009).
7. Adrian and Shin (2009).

Chapter Two: Origins of the Present System

1. Sprague (1910) is the classic account of pre-Fed crisis. For the post-Fed period I rely mainly on the account of Wood (2005), but other

classic histories of the Fed include Harding (1925), Wicker (1966), Timberlake (1993), D'Arista (1994), and Meltzer (2009).

2. Young (1999 [1924], 304).

3. Federal Reserve Act, section 13(2), "Discount of Commercial, Agricultural and Industrial Paper."

4. The origin of this adaptation is Charles F. Dunbar (1885), but the main advocate for this position at the time of the founding of the Fed was Laurence Laughlin (1903), and his student Henry Parker Willis (1914). See Mehrling (1997, 33–39).

5. Moulton (1918, 723). Moulton is the origin of the shiftability hypothesis, but see also Mitchell (1923, 1925) and Currie (1931).

6. Moulton (1918, 726).

7. Moulton (1918, 723 n. 1).

8. D'Arista (1994, chap. 1).

9. D'Arista (1994, 31–32).

10. Outside the Fed, other voices urged another version of quantitative control focused on the narrower goal of stabilizing an index of prices and on controlling the money supply (not the price of credit) in order to achieve that goal. The Yale economist Irving Fisher positioned himself as the intellectual leader of that movement (Fisher with Cohrsson 1934).

11. Laidler (1993).

12. Wicker (1969) coined the phrase *Strong rule*. See also Wood (2005, 206–208).

13. This rule can be understood as an adaptation, for American conditions, of classic British central banking practice. Because commercial loans played a less important role in the United States, open market operations to "make bank rate effective" were correspondingly more important than in Britain and not limited to times of exceptional slack.

14. For example, Warburg (1930).

15. Eichengreen (1992, chap. 7).

16. Wood (2005, 201) argues that, by the measure of the Strong rule, the Fed responded very aggressively, since it drove discounts down from $329 million in July 1929 to only $9 million in July 1930.

17. Friedman and Schwartz (1963). See also Currie (1934).

18. Fisher (1933). See also Hart (1938).

19. Phillips (1993) provides a useful history of the influence of these largely academic reformers on subsequent legislation. According to Sandilands (1990), the key policy actor was Lauchlin Currie, but see also Fisher (1935), Simons (1934), and Hart (1935).

20. Morton (1939, 281).

21. Morton (1939, 283).

22. Thus, Mints (1945) is beating a horse that had been dead for quite some time.

23. Laidler (1999) places Keynes in the larger context of developments in macroeconomic thought during the interwar period. Mehrling (1997) shows how the reception of Keynes in America was importantly conditioned by the indigenous intellectual tradition of institutionalism.

24. Hansen (1938, 318).

25. Wood (2005, 226).

26. Hetzel and Leach (2001a, 2001b). See also the biography of Martin (Bremner 2004).

Chapter Three: The Age of Management

1. Quoted in Sproul (1980, 53).

2. The increase happened in three steps: August 15, 1936; March 1, 1937; and May 1, 1937.

3. Keynes (1930, 2:143), Hicks (1939, 146–147).

4. Federal Open Market Committee (1952); and see Wood (2005, 247–252).

5. Sproul (1980, 105–111).

6. Brunner and Meltzer (1964) offer an influential critique of this procedure.

7. Sproul (1980, 155).

8. Sproul (1980, 160).

9. See Friedman (1959). Notwithstanding his role in the unfolding drama, Friedman himself is best understood, not through the lens of

Irving Fisher, but rather through that of Henry Simons (1934) and his proposal for 100 percent money. See Friedman (1948).

10. Debreu (1959), Arrow and Hahn (1971), Hahn (1965). I thank Douglas Gale (1982) for first bringing my attention to the importance of this problem, almost three decades ago when I was his student at the London School of Economics.

11. Marschak explicitly recognized Hicks (1935) as a precursor.

12. Other early attempts to reprise the Marschak approach include Modigliani (1944) and Patinkin (1956).

13. Tobin (1969, 26).

14. Friedman and Meiselman (1963), Ando and Modigliani (1965).

15. Ando and Modigliani (1969).

16. Tobin (1969, 26).

17. Minsky (1982, 1986), and see Mehrling (1999). Other voices include Fand and Scott (1958), Leijonhufvud (1968), Clower (1984), Goodhart (1975b), Kindleberger (1978), and Hicks (1989) in his late work.

Chapter Four: The Art of the Swap

1. Stigum and Crescenzi (2007, 869–873).

2. As early as 1913, Keynes used UIP to analyze the foreign exchange relationship between the British pound and the Indian rupee (Keynes 1913). Here is the origin of his later thoughts on forward interest parity (1923, 124) and normal backwardation (1930, 2:143).

3. Typically, but not always, this bet involves borrowing at a low rate in one currency and lending at a high rate in another, and the bet is called a "carry trade" because of the positive "carry" involved in the interest differential.

4. Operation Twist was followed by other increasingly inventive attempts to have it both ways until 1971, when, under President Nixon, the dollar was devalued against gold, and then, in 1973, allowed to float freely. From then on, UIP arbitrage continued, but without any offi-

cial support of the exchange value of the dollar to act as an anchor for expectations.

5. Black (1970, 5).

6. Here I follow Duffie and Singleton (2003, 180).

7. The reliable availability of this hedge is the reason that interest rate swap contracts are most typically written in terms of the London interbank offered rate (LIBOR) rather than Treasury rates. The availability of deep markets in Treasury securities of multiple maturities means that there is always liquidity in the related Treasury forward and futures contracts, which can also be used to hedge. But because interest rate swaps reference LIBOR, not the Treasury rate, the hedge is not perfect. It is possible to manage the remaining "basis risk" by trading the so-called TED (Treasury-Eurodollar) spread, which therefore becomes a sensitive indicator of systemwide stress.

8. The lack of a natural hedge is a key obstacle in the way of current proposals to move CDSs onto an exchange.

9. Sharpe (1964). See Mehrling (2005) for the fuller story, which is a case of multiple invention involving John Lintner at Harvard and also Jack Treynor.

10. More precisely, the key issue was whether the risk involved in EH and UIP arbitrage is diversifiable or not, an issue that was understood as a matter of covariance risk with the market as a whole.

11. Goodhart (1975a).

12. Friedman (1968), Phelps (1968).

13. Lucas (1976).

14. The Lucas critique was aimed directly at the Marschak-Tobin framework, and Tobin responded in kind, characterizing Lucas's quietist position as Monetarism Mark II (Tobin 1980), thus painting it as the successor to Milton Friedman's Monetarism Mark I. In fact, however, Friedman had never questioned the countercyclical project, and had confined his critique of Keynesian economic management to the question of which lever to use (monetary versus fiscal) and how best to use it (rules versus discretion).

Chapter Five: What Do Dealers Do?

1. But see Mehrling (2010b).

2. One reason for the development of credit rating agencies was to facilitate this kind of operation. See Flandreau, Gaillard, and Packer (2009).

3. Brunnermeier and Pedersen (2009). The following analysis takes its inspiration from the finance literature on market microstructure, especially Treynor (1987), Harris (2003), and Biais, Glosten, and Spatt (2005). See also Hicks (1989).

4. Adrian and Shin (2009).

5. This argument can be made more rigorous by assuming that the dealer hedges interest rate risk exposure in the interest rate futures market. See Mehrling (2010b).

6. Woodford and Curdia (2009).

7. Taylor and Woodford (1999).

Chapter Six: Learning from the Crisis

1. Federal Reserve, flow of funds statistics, available at www.federareserve.gov/releases/z1. Author's calculation.

2. ABCP was important for the off–balance sheet structured investment vehicles, a version of shadow banking in which Citibank was a dominant player. RP was more important for on–balance sheet arbitrage, a version of shadow banking in which the Union Bank of Switzerland was a dominant player.

3. Gorton (2010) provides the definitive account of the crisis from this perspective.

4. Gorton and Metrick (2009). Fed policy reactions during 2008 are well documented in Federal Reserve Bank of New York (2009).

5. Adrian, Kimbrough, and Marchioni (2010).

6. McGuire and von Peter (2009), Goldberg, Kennedy, and Miu (2010).

7. Hedge funds used money market funding indirectly, since they relied on loans from their prime brokers, who typically funded the loans with wholesale money market borrowing.

8. At the initial offering, credit rating agencies played a role in establishing price by putting their AAA imprimatur on the top tranches. But they did not buy or sell in support of those prices, either initially or in the secondary market.

9. Indeed, at the peak, some investment banks apparently used this synthetic CDO mechanism not merely to hedge credit protection that they had sold to clients, but even more to establish a net short position before the crash. That, of course, is not matched book; it is speculation, not dealing.

10. Tett (2009) tells the story of how J. P. Morgan first developed this system for corporate bonds and corporate CDSs. Bank for International Settlements (2008) tells how the system was adapted to securitized consumer loans and mortgages.

11. TSLF operated through periodic auctions, but the size of the auctions was scaled to the need, and everyone knew it. This is the sense in which the facility could be considered "standing."

12. The main beneficiaries were Societé Générale and Goldman Sachs. See SIGTARP (2009).

13. I had been concerned about the lack of public backstop for CDSs since the early days of the crisis (see Mehrling 2010a). On September 23, 2008, I published a letter in the Financial Times urging the Treasury to step in as "market maker of last resort in the index credit default swaps on the ABX." This is the seed of the idea later developed with my coauthors Kotlikoff and Milne under the name "credit insurer of last resort" (Kotlikoff and Mehrling 2008; Mehrling and Milne 2008). The key idea, however, was always to ensure shiftability by providing a liquidity backstop, not to socialize private losses of wealth. "Dealer of last resort" is therefore a better descriptor than "credit insurer of last resort." A related, but not identical, set of proposals was put forward early on in the crisis by Buiter and Sibert (2007).

14. Davis, McAndrews, and Franklin (2010).

15. Ashcraft, Malz, and Pozsar (2010).

References

Adrian, Tobias, Karin Kimbrough, and Dina Marchioni. 2010. "The Commercial Paper Funding Facility." Conference presentation, Society of Government Economists, Atlanta, January 4.

Adrian, Tobias, and Hyun Song Shin. 2009. "Money, Liquidity, and Monetary Policy." *American Economic Review* 99 (2): 600–605.

Ando, Albert, and Franco Modigliani. 1965. "The Relative Stability of Monetary Velocity and the Investment Multiplier." *American Economic Review* 55 (4): 693–728.

———. 1969. "Econometric Analysis of Stabilization Policies." *American Economic Review* 59 (2): 296–314.

Arrow, Kenneth, and Frank Hahn. 1971. *General Competitive Analysis*. San Francisco: Holden Day.

Ashcraft, Adam, Allan Malz, and Zoltan Pozsar. 2010. "The Term Asset-Backed Securities Facility." Conference presentation, Society of Government Economists, Atlanta, January 4.

Bagehot, Walter. 1906 [1873]. *Lombard Street: A Description of the Money Market*. New York: Charles Scribner's Sons.

Bank for International Settlements. 2008. "Credit Risk Transfers: Developments from 2005 to 2007." Basel Committee on Banking Supervision.

Biais, Bruno, Larry Glosten, and Chester Spatt. 2005. "Market Microstructure: A Survey of Microfoundations, Empirical Results, and Policy Implications." *Journal of Financial Markets* 8 (2): 217–264.

Black, Fischer. 1970. "Fundamentals of Liquidity." Mimeograph, Associates in Finance, June.

Borio, Claudio, and William White. 2004. "Whither Monetary and Financial Stability? The Implications of Evolving Policy Regimes." BIS Working Paper No. 147, Bank for International Settlements, February.

Bremner, Robert P. 2004. *Chairman of the Fed: William McChesney Martin, Jr., and the Creation of the Modern American Financial System.* New Haven, CT: Yale University Press.

Brunner, Karl, and Allan H. Meltzer. 1964. *The Federal Reserve's Attachment to the Free Reserves Concept.* Washington, DC: House Committee on Banking and Currency.

Brunnermeier, Markus, and Lasse Pedersen. 2009. "Market Liquidity and Funding Liquidity." *Review of Financial Studies* 22 (6): 2201–2233.

Buiter, Willem H., and Anne C. Sibert. 2007. "The Central Bankers as Market Maker of Last Resort." *Financial Times Maverecon,* August 12.

Clower, Robert W. 1984. *Money and Markets.* Cambridge: Cambridge University Press.

Currie, Lauchlin. 1931. "The Decline of the Commercial Loan." *Quarterly Journal of Economics* 45 (4): 698–709.

———. 1934. *The Supply and Control of Money in the United States.* Cambridge, MA: Harvard University Press.

D'Arista, Jane W. 1994. *Federal Reserve Monetary Policy: 1915–1935.* Armonk, NY: M. E. Sharpe.

Davis, Jeanmarie, Jamie McAndrews, and Kathryn Franklin. 2010. "The Money Market Investor Funding Facility." Conference presentation, Society of Government Economists, Atlanta, January 4.

Debreu, Gerard. 1959. *Theory of Value.* New York: Wiley.

Duffie, D., and K. J. Singleton. 2003. *Credit Risk; Pricing, Measurement, and Management.* Princeton, NJ: Princeton University Press.

Dunbar, Charles F. 1885. *Chapters on Banking.* Cambridge, MA: N.p.

Eichengreen, Barry. 1992. *Golden Fetters: The Gold Standard and the Great Depression,* 1919–1939. New York: Oxford University Press.

Fand, David I., and Ira O. Scott, Jr. 1958. "The Federal Reserve System's 'Bills Only' Policy: A Suggested Interpretation." *Journal of Business* 31 (1): 12–18.

Federal Open Market Committee, Federal Reserve System. 1952. "Federal Open Market Committee Report of Ad Hoc Subcommittee on the Government Securities Market." Reprinted in U.S. House Committee on Banking and Currency, *The Federal Reserve System after Fifty Years: Hearings before the Subcommittee on Domestic Finance of the Committee on Banking and Currency*, vol. 3. 88th Congress, 2nd session. Washington, DC: U.S. Government Printing Office, 1964.

Federal Reserve Bank of New York. 2009. *Domestic Open Market Operations during 2008*. New York: Federal Reserve Bank of New York.

Fisher, Irving. 1911. The Purchasing Power of Money. New York: Macmillan.

———. 1933. "The Debt-Deflation Theory of Great Depressions." *Econometrica* 1 (4): 337–357.

———. 1935. *100% Money*. New York: Adelphi.

Fisher, Irving, with Hans R. L. Cohrsson. 1934. *Stable Money: A History of the Movement*. New York: Adelphi.

Flandreau, Marc, Norbert Gaillard, and Frank Packer. 2009. "Ratings Performance, Regulation and the Great Depression: Lessons from Government Securities." DP 7328, Center for Economic Policy Research, June.

Friedman, Milton. 1948. "A Monetary and Fiscal Framework for Economic Stability." *American Economic Review* 38 (3): 245–264.

———. 1959. *A Program for Monetary Stability*. New York: Fordham University Press.

———. 1968. "The Role of Monetary Policy." *American Economic Review* 58 (1): 1–17.

Friedman, Milton, and D. Meiselman. 1963. "The Relative Stability of Monetary Velocity and the Investment Multiplier in the United States, 1897–1958." In *Stabilization Policies*, by Commission on Money and Credit. Englewood Cliffs, NJ: Prentice-Hall.

Friedman, Milton, and Anna J. Schwartz. 1963. *A Monetary History of the United States, 1863–1960*. Princeton, NJ: Princeton University Press.

Gale, Douglas. 1982. *Money: In Equilibrium*. Cambridge: Cambridge University Press.

Goldberg, Linda, Craig Kennedy, and Jason Miu. 2010. "FX Swap Lines and Dollar Funding Costs." Conference presentation, Society of Government Economists, Atlanta, January 4.

Goodhart, Charles A. E. 1975a. "Monetary Relationships: A View from Threadneedle Street." Reserve Bank of Australia, *Papers in Monetary Economics* 1.

————. 1975b. *Money, Information, and Uncertainty*. London: Macmillan.

Gorton, Gary B. 2010. *Slapped by the Invisible Hand: The Panic of 2007*. Financial Management Association Survey and Synthesis. New York: Oxford University Press.

Gorton, Gary, and Andrew Metrick. 2009. "Securitized Banking and the Run on Repo." Yale ICF Working Paper no. 09-14, Yale University.

Gurley, John G., and Edward S. Shaw. 1960. *Money in a Theory of Finance*. Washington, DC: Brookings Institution.

Hahn, Frank. 1965. "On Some Problems of Proving the Existence of an Equilibrium in a Monetary Economy." In *Theory of Interest Rates*, edited by F. Hahn and F. Brechling. London: Macmillan.

Hansen, Alvin H. 1938. *Full Recovery or Stagnation?* New York: Norton.

Harding, W.P.G. 1925. *The Formative Period of the Federal Reserve System (During the World Crisis)*. Boston: Houghton Mifflin.

Harris, Larry. 2003. *Trading and Exchanges: Market Microstructure for Practitioners*. New York: Oxford University Press.

Hart, Albert G. 1935. "The 'Chicago Plan' of Banking Reform." *Review of Economic Studies* 2 (2): 104–116.

————. 1938. *Debts and Recovery*. New York: Twentieth Century Fund.

Hawtrey, Ralph G. 1923. *Currency and Credit*. 2nd edition. London: Longmans, Green & Co.

————. 1934. *The Art of Central Banking*. London: Longmans, Green & Co.

Hetzel, Robert L., and Ralph F. Leach. 2001a. "After the Accord: Reminiscences on the Birth of the Modern Fed." Federal Reserve Bank of Richmond, *Economic Quarterly* 87 (winter): 57–64.

———. 2001b. "The Treasury-Fed Accord: A New Narrative Account." Federal Reserve Bank of Richmond, *Economic Quarterly* 87 (winter): 33–55.

Hicks, John R. 1935. "A Suggestion for Simplifying the Theory of Money." *Economica*, new series, 2 (5): 1–19.

———. 1937. "Mr. Keynes and the 'Classics': A Suggested Interpretation." *Econometrica* 5 (2): 147–159.

———. 1939. *Value and Capital*. Oxford: Clarendon Press.

———. 1989. *A Market Theory of Money*. Oxford: Clarendon Press.

Jones, Jesse H., with Edward Angly. 1951. *Fifty Billion Dollars: My Thirteen Years with the RFC, 1932–1945*. New York: Macmillan.

Keynes, John Maynard. 1913. *Indian Currency and Finance*. London: Macmillan.

———. 1923. *A Tract on Monetary Reform*. London: Macmillan.

———. 1930. *A Treatise on Money*. 2 vols. London: Macmillan.

———. 1936. *The General Theory of Employment, Interest, and Money*. New York: Harcourt, Brace.

Kindleberger, Charles P. 1978. *Manias, Panics, and Crashes: A History of Financial Crises*. New York: Basic Books.

Kotlikoff, Laurence J. 2010. *Jimmy Stewart Is Dead: Ending the World's Ongoing Plague with Limited Purpose Banking*. Hoboken, NJ: John Wiley & Sons.

Kotlikoff, Larry, and Perry Mehrling. 2008. "Bagehot plus RFC: The Right Financial Fix." *Financial Times*, September 25, Economist Forum.

Laidler, David E. W. 1993. "Hawtrey, Harvard, and the Origins of the Chicago Tradition." *Journal of Political Economy* 101 (6): 1068–1103.

———. 1999. *Fabricating the Keynesian Revolution: Studies in the Interwar Literature on Money, the Cycle, and Unemployment*. Cambridge: Cambridge University Press.

Laughlin, J. Laurence. 1903. *Principles of Money*. New York: Scribner's.

Leijonhufvud, Axel. 1968. *On Keynesian Economics and the Economics of Keynes: A Study in Monetary Theory*. New York: Oxford University Press.

Lucas, Robert E. 1976. "Econometric Policy Evaluation: A Critique." In *The Phillips Curve and Labor Markets*, edited by Karl Brunner and Allan H. Meltzer. Carnegie-Rochester Conference Series on Public Policy, vol. 1. Amsterdam: North-Holland.

Markowitz, Harry. 1952. "Portfolio Selection." *Journal of Finance* 7 (1): 77–91.

Marschak, Jacob. 1938. "Money and the Theory of Assets." *Econometrica* 6 (4): 311–325.

McGuire, Patrick, and Goetz von Peter. 2009. "The US Dollar Shortage in Global Banking." Bank for International Settlements, *Quarterly Review* (March): 47–60.

Mehrling, Perry. 1997. *The Money Interest and the Public Interest: American Monetary Thought, 1920–1970*. Cambridge, MA: Harvard University Press.

———. 1999. "The Vision of Hyman P. Minsky." *Journal of Economic Behavior and Organization* 39 (2): 129–158.

———. 2005. *Fischer Black and the Revolutionary Idea of Finance*. Hoboken, NJ: John Wiley & Sons.

———. 2010a. "Credit Default Swaps: The Key to Financial Reform." In *Time for a Visible Hand: Lessons from the 2008 World Financial Crisis*, edited by Stephany Griffith-Jones, Jose Antonio O'Campo, and Joseph E. Stiglitz. New York: Oxford University Press.

———. 2010b. "Monetary Implementation Policy: A Microstructure Approach." In *David Laidler's Contributions to Macroeconomics*, edited by Robert Leeson. London: Palgrave Macmillan.

Mehrling, Perry, and Alistair Milne. 2008. "Government's Role as Credit Insurer of Last Resort and How It Can Be Fulfilled." Cass Business School, Centre for Banking Research, Working Paper 01-2008, October 29.

Meltzer, Allan H. 2009. *A History of the Federal Reserve*. Chicago: University of Chicago Press.

Minsky, Hyman P. 1957. "Central Banking and Money Market Changes." *Quarterly Journal of Economics* 71 (2): 171–187.

———. 1967. "Financial Intermediation in the Money and Capital Markets." In *Issues in Banking and Monetary Analysis*, edited by

G. Pontecorvo, R. P. Shay, and A. G. Hart. New York: Holt, Rinehart, and Winston.

―――. 1982. *Could "It" Happen Again? Essays on Instability and Finance*. Armonk, NY: M. E. Sharpe.

―――. 1986. *Stabilizing an Unstable Economy*. New Haven, CT: Yale University Press.

Mints, Lloyd. 1945. *A History of Banking Theory in Great Britain and the United States*. Chicago: University of Chicago Press.

Mitchell, Waldo. 1923. "The Institutional Basis for the Shiftability Theory of Bank Liquidity." University of Chicago, *Journal of Business* 1 (3): 334–356.

―――. 1925. *The Uses of Bank Funds*. Chicago: University of Chicago Press.

Modigliani, Franco. 1944. "Liquidity Preference and the Theory of Interest and Money." *Econometrica* 12 (1): 45–88.

Morris, Charles R. 2008. *The Trillion Dollar Meltdown: Easy Money, High Rollers, and the Great Credit Crash*. New York: Public Affairs.

Morton, Walter A. 1939. "Liquidity and Solvency." *American Economic Review* 29 (2): 272–285.

Moulton, H. G. 1918. "Commercial Banking and Capital Formation." *Journal of Political Economy* 26 (5, 6, 7, 9): 484–508, 638–663, 705–731, 849–881.

Patinkin, Don. 1956. *Money, Interest, and Prices: An Integration of Monetary and Value Theory*. Evanston, IL: Row, Peterson, & Co.

Phelps, Edmund S. 1968. "Money Wage Dynamics and Labor Market Equilibrium." *Journal of Political Economy* 76 (4, part 2): 687–711.

Phillips, Ronnie J. 1993. *The Chicago Plan and New Deal Banking Reform*. Armonk, NY: M. E. Sharpe.

Sandilands, Roger J. 1990. *The Life and Political Economy of Lauchlin Currie*. Durham, NC: Duke University Press.

Sayers, Richard S. 1936. *Bank of England Operations, 1890–1914*. London: P. S. King & Sons.

Schumpeter, Joseph A. 1934. *The Theory of Economic Development: An Inquiry into Profits, Capital, Credit, Interest, and the Business Cycle*. Cambridge, MA: Harvard University Press.

Sharpe, William. 1964. "Capital Asset Prices: A Theory of Market Equilibrium under Conditions of Risk." *Journal of Finance* 19 (3): 425–442.

Shiller, Robert J. 2008. *The Subprime Solution: How Today's Global Financial Crisis Happened, and What to Do about It*. Princeton, NJ: Princeton University Press.

SIGTARP [Special Inspector General for the Troubled Asset Relief Program]. 2009. *Factors Affecting Efforts to Limit Payments to AIG Counterparties*. Washington, DC: Government Printing Office.

Simons, Henry C. 1934. *A Positive Program for Laissez-Faire*. Chicago: University of Chicago Press.

Sprague, Oliver M. W. 1910. *History of Crises under the National Banking System*. Fairfield, NJ: Augustus Kelley, 1977.

Sproul, Allan. 1980. *Selected Papers of Allan Sproul*. Edited by Lawrence S. Ritter. New York: Federal Reserve Bank of New York.

Stigum, Marcia, and Anthony Crescenzi. 2007. *Stigum's Money Market*. 4th ed. New York: McGraw-Hill.

Taylor, John B. 2009. *Getting Off Track: How Government Actions and Interventions Caused, Prolonged, and Worsened the Financial Crisis*. Stanford, CA: Hoover Institution Press.

Taylor, John B., and Michael Woodford. 1999. *Handbook of Macroeconomics*. 3 vols. New York: Elsevier.

Tett, Gillian. 2009. *Fool's Gold: How the Bold Dream of a Small Tribe at J. P. Morgan Was Corrupted by Wall Street Greed and Unleashed Catastrophe*. New York: Free Press.

Timberlake, Richard H. 1993. *Monetary Policy in the United States: An Intellectual and Institutional History*. Chicago: University of Chicago Press.

Tobin, James. 1958. "Liquidity Preference as Behavior towards Risk." *Review of Economic Studies* 25 (2): 65–86.

———. 1969. "A General Equilibrium Approach to Money." *Journal of Money, Credit, and Banking* 1 (1): 15–29.

———. 1980. *Asset Accumulation and Economic Activity: Reflections on Contemporary Macroeconomic Theory*. Chicago: University of Chicago Press.

Treynor, Jack. 1987. "The Economics of the Dealer Function." *Financial Analysts Journal* 43 (6): 27–34.

Walras, Léon. 1954 [1926, 1874]. *Elements of Pure Economics, or the Theory of Social Wealth.* Translation by William Jaffe of definitive 1926 edition. Homewood, IL: Irwin. First edition published Lausanne: L. Corbaz & cie, 1874.

Warburg, Paul M. 1930. *The Federal Reserve System: Its Origin and Growth.* New York: Macmillan.

Wicker, Elmus. 1966. *Federal Reserve Monetary Policy, 1917–1933.* New York: Random House.

———. 1969. "Brunner and Meltzer on Federal Reserve Monetary Policy during the Great Depression." *Canadian Journal of Economics* 2 (2): 318–321.

Wicksell, Knut. 1936 [1898]. *Interest and Prices.* Translated by R. F. Kahn. London: Macmillan.

Willis, Henry Parker. 1914. "The Federal Reserve Act." *American Economic Review* 4 (1): 1–24.

Wood, John H. 2005. *A History of Central Banking in Great Britain and the United States.* Cambridge: Cambridge University Press.

Woodford, Michael. 2003. *Interest and Prices: Foundations of a Theory of Monetary Policy.* Princeton, NJ: Princeton University Press.

Woodford, Michael, and Vasco Curdia. 2009. "Credit Frictions and Optimal Monetary Policy." Discussion Paper no. 0910-01, Department of Economics, Columbia University.

Young, Allyn A. 1999 [1924]. "Mobilizing Bank Credits: Possibilities of the Federal Reserve." In *Money and Growth: Selected Essays of Allyn Young,* edited by Perry Mehrling and Roger Sandilands. London: Routledge.

Zandi, Mark M. 2009. *Financial Shock: A 360° Look at the Subprime Mortgage Implosion, and How to Avoid the Next Financial Crisis.* Upper Saddle River, NJ: FT Press.

Index

Milton Keynes UK
Ingram Content Group UK Ltd.
UKHW021833071224
451936UK00002B/11